BBC MUSIC GUIDES

DEBUSSY PIANO MUSIC

BBC MUSIC GUIDES

Debussy Piano Music

FRANK DAWES

UNIVERSITY OF WASHINGTON PRESS

SEATTLE

First published 1969 by the British Broadcasting Corporation
Copyright © Frank Dawes 1969
University of Washington Press edition first published 1971
Library of Congress Catalog Card Number 71 – 105438
Printed in England

INTRODUCTION

Debussy died in 1918, just over fifty years ago. Today his reputation stands as high as ever it did. Igor Stravinsky, the doyen of
contemporary composers, can indeed say with truth, 'the musicians
of my generation and I myself owe the most to Debussy'. Although
some critics were prematurely writing him off in the 1920s, the
popularity with the general public of much of his music has never
been in question. That is particularly true of the piano music.
Mention the name of Debussy to the layman and nine times out of
ten it will be the piano compositions that first spring to his mind.
He will, of course, almost immediately recall certain of the great
orchestral pieces – the *Prélude à l'après-midi d'un faune*, *La Mer*, and
perhaps the orchestral *Images* and *Nocturnes*. Also he will recollect
that Debussy was the composer of a uniquely beautiful opera, and
somewhere at the end of the queue, unless he has had special
reasons for cultivating such things, will come certain of the songs,
probably those to Verlaine texts. But the piano music will be in the
forefront of his mind, a circumstance that underlines the fact that
Debussy is indisputably one of the select body of composers who
have enlarged the piano repertoire not merely in the quantitative
sense of composing a corpus of fine music for the instrument, but
also in the qualitative sense of adding a new dimension to that
particular branch of music. Debussy did this, of course, in all the
many departments of music to which he addressed himself. In the
field of the piano he developed new techniques that themselves
grew out of his highly original and personal attitudes to chords and
harmony. In particular his harmony, with its often shifting, evanes-
cent clouds of sound, with chords melting and merging into each
other, disappearing and regrouping in endlessly subtle ways, in-
volved a completely new appraisal of the functions of the pedals.

Debussy's music, despite the enormous amount written in eluci-
dation, is still surrounded by mystery and paradox. Particularly
paradoxical is the situation in regard to the piano music. How did
it come about that Debussy arrived at a fully mature pianoforte
style, a style that embodies all that is vital and essential to the
composer – what, in a word, we would describe as Debussyan –
only in 1903 with the *Estampes* twenty-three years after his earliest

5

known piano piece and only twelve before his last? During those earlier twenty-three years Debussy had composed a large proportion of his most important songs, including representative settings of poems by Baudelaire, Mallarmé and especially Verlaine, and had composed in the 1890s that utterly Debussyan orchestral evocation of the poem which is the very quintessence of the *symboliste* movement, Mallarmé's *L'après-midi d'un faune*, as well as the orchestral *Nocturnes* and the String Quartet. *La Mer* was begun in 1903 and *Pelléas et Mélisande* had been brought to completion in the preceding year. These works in other media are among Debussy's very greatest creations. Had Debussy's career ended there, and had his piano output consisted of no more than a bundle of rather superior salon pieces and the more significant, if as yet only prophetic *Pour le piano* (completed in 1901), his reputation would have been secure, though it would have presented one less facet to the world and Debussy would not today be seriously regarded as a composer for the piano. Into the one decade, 1903–13, were crowded all the so-called impressionistic piano pieces, and by 1915 he had, with the *Douze études* and *En blanc et noir* for two pianos, moved somewhat away from the aural-visual concepts of musical impressionism.

It would seem that Debussy regarded piano composition as a not too important side-line up to about 1896, when he began work on *Pour le piano*. It is significant that his earliest success was as a song composer. Most of the early piano pieces have similar textures to the song accompaniments, a similarity that extends to the superimposition of plastic, rather fragile melodic lines like those in the songs. They are rarely of the quality of the songs, though it is again significant that among the best of them are those comprising the *Suite bergamasque*, in which Debussy attempted to evoke, in terms of the piano, the nostalgia of the vanished world of Verlaine's *Fêtes galantes*. One of the most perceptive critics, Wilfred Mellers, has in fact argued persuasively that the songs are the key to Debussy's most interesting music.[1] They are 'the music of *Fantôme* and of Pierrot', in which the image is often more real than the object. Mellers sees the continuation of the songs, not in the impressionist piano pieces, wherein Debussy's music 'lost control and

[1] The Final Works of Claude Debussy, *Music and Letters*, vol. xx (London, 1947).

restraint, its serene, smiling wistfulness and became a tissue of nerves and sense organs, but in the orchestral works and *Pelléas*, where the same modes of sensibility and the same techniques are present'. That is a personal view to which by no means all of Debussy's admirers would whole-heartedly subscribe, but it goes some way towards accounting for the 'serene, smiling wistfulness' and the plastic melodic lines of the *Suite bergamasque*.

Mystery of another kind is of the essence of Debussy's music. He was throughout his career concerned with the crystallisation of dreams into sound. In a paper read to the Royal Musical Association,[1] Edward Lockspeiser traced the origins of Debussy's preoccupation with dreams to his interest in the more visionary of Turner's paintings, especially the remarkable seascapes which have their parallels in *La Mer* and other sea pieces, and in the writings of Poe with their dark, suggestive symbolism. Debussy's dream-world early encompassed the world of the *commedia dell'arte*, preserved with overtones of melancholy in the paintings of Watteau and nostalgically recreated in the poems of Verlaine that Debussy himself set. Debussy's closest friends and associates throughout his life were not his fellow musicians, but poets and painters, especially those of the symbolist and impressionist schools, whose aims and artistic tenets he largely shared. Mallarmé was quite early in his career able to write, 'I have found an intimate and peculiar manner of depicting and setting down very fugitive impressions', and found himself frightened at the task of weaving them together 'as in a symphony'. As Mallarmé's comment would imply, poetry for him aspired to the condition of music, just as it did for the other symbolist poets and just as painting did for the impressionist painters. The words could as well have been written about Debussy's piano music of 1903–13. By then Debussy was 'setting down very fugitive impressions' from all sorts of sources. Lockspeiser recalls Cézanne's comment concerning Monet, 'whose art had been reduced to an accurate rendering of optical sensations, that "he is nothing but an eye"', and neatly remarks that 'of Debussy it may be said, in the same superior sense, that he is nothing but an ear'. A point of contact between Debussy and Monet and his colleagues may be made, though Debussy disliked the term

[1] 'Debussy's concept of the Dream', *Proceedings of the Royal Musical Association*, vol. 89 (1962–3).

'impressionist' as applied to his music, feeling himself to be nearer to the symbolist poets. The sheen over some Monet paintings suggests a consciousness on the part of the painter of the space between him and the object of his painting, a space that may be filled with dust particles, with mist, or even with raindrops, any of which refract light rays and bring about a view of the object that is true for the moment (hence Monet's extraordinary haste when painting) but which may change in character ever and anon. The object may be seen hazily, slightly distorted, or even with perfect clarity, but the essential fact is that the object is seen through the atmosphere and that the impression is necessarily a fleeting one. One feels that Debussy, especially in his impressionist piano pieces, picked up sounds from the atmosphere in very much the same way. Not only do we get from him a variety of different sounds from different sources, a kind of counterpoint of subject-matter in one and the same piece (e.g. *La sérénade interrompue*), but he shows a keen ear and a keen appreciation of the way sounds reverberate in the atmosphere around him. It is a well-known fact that no musical sound is a pure single note, any one note sends out a whole series of harmonics or overtones above its fundamental, stronger or weaker according to the agent producing the sound. Among such agents, brass instruments and bells produce very strong overtones. If one stands very near to a belfry, the impression of chimes borne upon one's ears includes a perpetually sounding complex chord hanging on the air, somewhere in the midst of which the bells are adding to the confusion – a very different thing from the clear sound of bells heard at half-a-mile's distance, most of the harmonics having faded *en route*. Debussy caught the sound of bells and their overtones supremely well in *La Cathédrale engloutie* (around bar 20) and much of his harmony was derived from his knowledge of acoustics. Such chords as

Ex. 1

make perfect acoustical sense given the presupposition of a far-off fundamental, often too deep to hear even in the imagination.

Debussy's dream-world, beginning with the figures of the *commedia dell'arte* was soon to include a variety of regions, some known to him at first hand, some largely by intuition reinforced by some purely musical acquaintance. Recurring subjects in his piano music are mostly exotic in so far as they belong outside the normal day-to-day run of his Parisian existence. Sometimes the escape is no farther than into the countryside near Paris where he can watch the clouds sailing across the sky, hear and feel the wind across the plain, or muse pensively on the dead leaves carpeting the woodlands. In one of the most memorable of his articles he explains his absence from a certain Sunday concert he should have been reporting:

> I had lingered in autumn-filled landscapes, bound by the spell of ancient forests. The golden leaves, as they fell from the agonised trees, and the shrill Angelus bell, bidding the fields take their sleep, sent up a sweet, persuasive voice that counselled complete forgetfulness. In solitary state the sun sank to rest. Not a single peasant was there to strike a stereotyped attitude in the foreground. Beasts and men went quietly homewards, their humble task accomplished whose beauty had this advantage, that it invited neither praise nor blame . . . How far away were those discussions on art in which the names of great men sometimes sound like swear-words! . . . Never, perhaps, did I love music more than at this period when I never heard it mentioned . . .[1]

Other regions in Debussy's dream-world are geographically farther afield. In 1889 he was most impressed by the Javanese and Annamite *gamelan* orchestras consisting of a single string instrument, a flute and a variety of gongs and bells delicately struck with thickly padded sticks. Their pentatonic music and distinctive sonorities were later evoked in *Pagodes* and other pieces with oriental settings. Spain, too, especially Andalusia with its music and architecture showing strong Moorish influences, was geographically as remote from Debussy's experience. Yet his intuition led him infallibly to the very heart of the Spanish idiom, so infallibly that Falla considered *Soirée dans Grenade* of all piano pieces the most fully expressive of the Andalusian scene. Nearer home was the music-

[1] Translations of Debussy's writings are taken from *The Theories of Claude Debussy*, by Léon Vallas translated by Maire O'Brien (London, 1929).

hall, productive of some of the most sharply defined and amusing of Debussy's piano pieces, and even more remote were the pagan gods, especially Pan, who is not only met in person but reincarnated in Mallarmé's faun.

Such then, in brief, was Debussy's world. As he himself said in an interview in about 1911:

Every sound you hear around you can be reproduced. Everything that a keen ear perceives in the rhythm of the surrounding world can be represented musically. To some people rules are of primary importance. But my desire is to reproduce only what I hear.

Debussy's respect for rules was not very great, and it would be difficult to reduce his aurally guided procedures to a hard-and-fast method. Analysis can tell us what the ingredients are, but does little to explain the ultimate mystery of his supreme skill in composing such a wonderful series of evocations of sights, sounds and even perfumes and memories. He himself abhorred musical analysis. In 1913 he wrote in *Gil Blas*:

Let us maintain that the beauty of a work of art must always remain mysterious; that is to say, it is impossible to explain exactly how it is created. Let us at all costs preserve this magic peculiar to music, for of all the arts it is the most susceptible to magic . . . In the name of all the gods, let us not attempt to destroy or explain it.

And eight years earlier he had said:

There is too much *writing* of music. Too much importance attached to . . . the formula, the craft.

Something has already been said concerning the nature of certain of Debussy's chords (see Ex. 1). As early as 1889, Debussy was arguing with his former teacher Guiraud about the validity of chains of successive chords which, whether concords or discords, tended to move in similar parallel motion, and the conversations and the chords were carefully noted down by young Maurice Emmanuel.[1] Debussy's arguments embodied an entirely new concept: that

[1] They are reproduced complete in Lockspeiser's *Debussy, his life and mind*, vol. I (London, 1962).

discords are complete and final entities that demand no resolution on to a concord. The following bar is typical of innumerable such things in his music:

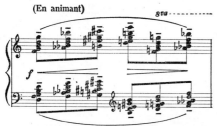

Ex. 2   (La terrasse des audiences au clair de lune)

(En animant)

Technically this quotation consists of one chord – constituted like the familiar dominant seventh – in a number of different keys. Yet it is plain that its use here has nothing in common with a harmony textbook dominant seventh; it exists for its own sake, not in relation to a tonic chord of resolution. Debussy frequently used old chords in new ways, even so simple a chord as the common major triad:

Ex. 3

(Modéré)   (Minstrels)

Such free-ranging tonal adventures do not imply the destruction of tonality, though they bring about a weakening of the old magnetic poles (tonic, dominant and subdominant), the relationship between which is extremely tenuous in Debussy's mature music. Ex. 3, which is really in G major, only hints at that relationship in the last two chords of the quotation. It also points not only to Debussy's use of consecutives in general (and any interval or bundle of intervals is likely to be used consecutively) but of fifths in particular, a feature that may have been taken by him from early medieval *organum*. The use of modes might derive from medieval plainsong too, though modal melodies were in the air in Debussy's young days – witness the earlier works of Gabriel Fauré. Debussy composed melodies with modal features for some of his earlier piano music, as we shall see later.

The influence on Debussy of the Javanese *gamelan* first shows itself in *Pagodes* of 1903, both in prevailingly pentatonic melodies and the bell-like sounds that accompany them:

Ex. 4   (Modérément animé)
dans une sonorité plus claire   (Pagodes)

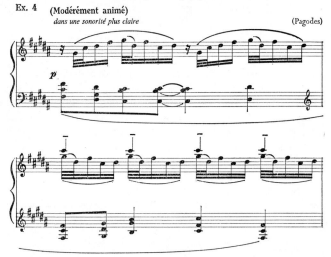

The pentatonic scales were only some of several, other than orthodox major and minor, used by Debussy. One such was the whole-tone scale which Debussy used freely in his piano music from *Pour le piano* onwards. Almost every bar of the mature Debussy contains examples of the infiltration of, to put it at its simplest, the scale of C major by the black keys, of the coexistence of major and minor thirds, of a near-permanent tonal ambiguity that, together with the supplest of rhythmic patterns, gives his music an almost unrivalled flexibility. His original view of music's elements enabled him to forge tools for the realisation of his dreams and imaginings. To them we owe the existence of a body of music that is evocative, poetic, colourful, beautiful and above all unique.

II

1880–1901

The piano works of Debussy's earliest period are for the most part orthodox in both their formal design and their harmonic language. Many of the pieces are not much more than superior salon music, though their superiority over most things of their kind emanating from *fin-de-siècle* Paris could be stressed. Many of them are beautifully fashioned and charming. Perhaps the whole of Debussy's piano music before *Pour le piano* has been too readily condemned as unrepresentative and unimportant, for the determined seeker will be rewarded with a few hints of things to come and a few parallels with the contemporary songs. Before considering the individual pieces, it is worth tracing briefly the sources of Debussy's early piano style, even though some of them had served their purpose and been duly discarded by the time the composer reached pianistic maturity.

Martin Cooper listed some of the models for the early piano music:[1]

The ... *Deux Arabesques* and *Petite Suite* reveal ... a Debussy still touched by the popular favourites of the day – Benjamin Godard, Massenet, Saint-Saëns and, above all, Grieg, whose influence appears also in the *Suite bergamasque*, much of which also dates from this period of Debussy's production.

And he might have added the name of Delibes, the composer of elegant ballets. But certain other of Debussy's piano pieces of the 1890s show traces of wider influence. In 1880 he was private musician in the household of Nadezhda von Meck, Tchaikovsky's benefactress, both in Russia and on her travels in Italy and Switzerland, and he visited her again in Moscow the following year. His very earliest piano piece, *Danse bohémienne*, is Tchaikovskian in a mild way, and his knowledge of Borodin's songs is reflected in the melodic lines of a number of pieces. Mussorgsky's *Boris Godunov* seems to have been first brought to his notice (at first without much effect) in 1889, the year of the Universal Exhibition in Paris when he not only heard Javanese music but refreshed his memory of Russian music at two orchestral concerts devoted mainly to the works of the nationalists. In 1889, too, he travelled to Bayreuth where he heard *Tristan* for the first time, as well as

[1] *French Music from the death of Berlioz to the death of Fauré* (London, 1951).

Parsifal and *Die Meistersinger* for the second. He soon discovered that Wagner's methods were not for him, but he expressed admiration for Wagner's works, especially *Tristan* and *Parsifal* on a number of occasions. *Parsifal* he described as 'one of the most beautiful monuments ever raised to music; incomparable and bewildering, splendid and strong', and there is no doubt that a great deal in both these operas sank deeply into his consciousness. The early Baudelaire songs show a fairly obvious response to Wagner, and *Pelléas et Mélisande* in its totally different way a more subtle one both harmonically and in the use of leitmotives. Even in the later *Le Martyre de Saint Sébastien* memories of *Parsifal* remain.

Debussy's first piano piece, the *Danse bohémienne* of 1880, significantly has an exotic setting, though the local colour is extremely pale when seen beside such masterly evocations of national music as the later Spanish pieces. In 2/4 time, the *Danse bohémienne* has a few touches of polka rhythm. There is also a mild gipsiness that may have been picked up from the gipsy singers at Moscow cabarets that Debussy is reputed to have frequented. In texture the piece has something of the salon style of Tchaikovsky, though very much simplified. Mme von Meck sent the manuscript to Tchaikovsky himself, writing, in a letter dated 8 September 1880, 'I would like to draw your attention to a short work by Debussy the pianist. The young man wants to devote himself entirely to composing; he writes really delightfully.' A month later Tchaikovsky replied, 'It's a very nice thing but really too short; not one thought is expressed to the end and the form is extremely messy and devoid of wholeness.' That is fair comment, if one accepts that the final section is unduly abbreviated. The only moment of distinction occurs in the coda, where a tonic chord (the piece is in B minor) over a submediant pedal-point gives prominence to the interval of a major seventh. The *Danse bohémienne* was not published until 1932.

Debussy's first published piano pieces were the well-known *Deux Arabesques* of 1888. 'Graceful reproductions of the ballet style of Delibes' (as Lockspeiser puts it), they show much more assurance, both in the matter of formal organisation and in pianistic resource. The first plays off triplet arabesques in descending sequence (as near a notated version of the song of the willow warbler as one could well imagine) against an even flow of left-hand quavers in broken-chord formations. The middle section grows out of a more reflective, songlike phrase culminating in a sturdy, chordal version in C major. The quick return from this key to the original E major is noteworthy. Chromatic alteration transforms the C major triad into a C sharp minor first inversion and the tonal shift has been accomplished most gracefully.

The second Arabesque is more capricious than the first, with a crisp, chirruping figure (again reminiscent of birdsong) dominating first and last sections and containing a comical pseudo-fugato in its coda, beginning as if for two bassoons. The latter part of the middle section again involves modulation and again the modulation is managed with charm and point. C major to the original G major presents no insuperable problems, but Debussy chooses a round-about route, plunging directly (a straw in the wind?) from the dominant seventh of C to the E major tonic chord. A sideslip into E flat major and an unprepared leap into G major complete a not too orthodox journey. There is much delicate pianistic writing, notably just before the *meno mosso* indication towards the end of the piece, and at the *meno mosso* itself comes the first example in Debussy's piano music of the composer's method of indicating the use of the sustaining pedal by notes of 'impossible' duration (impossible for the fingers, that is, and capable of being sustained only by the pedal). Here he writes *armonioso* as an added guide, and it seems likely that he would in later life have tied at least some of the bass semibreves into a second bar.

The *Petite Suite* for piano duet of 1889 inhabits the same world. Composed shortly after the *Ariettes oubliées* to poems by Verlaine, the *Suite* is in such sharp contrast to those remarkable songs that it could almost have come from another hand. Yet the *Suite*, helped by an orchestration by Henri Büsser, has become even more popular than the *Arabesques*. The spirit of Delibes is again the presiding genius, but, as Lockspeiser, Vallas and others have suggested, there is a nodding acquaintance with other of Debussy's contemporaries. *En bateau*, the first piece, floats a melody over a delicate broken-chord accompaniment, using a duet technique similar to that in the first piece in Fauré's *Dolly*, which it antici-pated by a few years, however. A short passage at the end of the middle section is prophetic in two ways: firstly in its use of the whole-tone scale: and secondly in the little pattern of semiquavers contributed by the *secondo* player, very like such things in the later music used to symbolise ripples, eddies and whirlpools in water:

Ex. 5

(Andantino)   (En bateau)

un peu retenu

Cortège, the second piece, has a fine swinging rhythm, even with a touch of brass band swagger about it here and there, some effective doubling of parts and some cleverly engineered modulations, especially at the end of the middle section. The *Menuet* is perhaps the gem of the set. Beautifully light-fingered, the disposition of parts shows great regard, especially, for the inner voices. The whole piece has a delicate perfection rare in Debussy's piano music at this time. It begins with suggestions of elfin pipes and horns, and the magical vanishing trick at the end, with dynamics reduced from *p* to *pppp*, has fairy horn-calls echoing faintly round the main melody in a way that suggests that Debussy's piano music was by now beginning to find a place in his unique dream-world. The final piece, *Ballet,* brings us down to earth again, for it goes off with a swagger that reminded Léon Vallas[1] of Chabrier's *Bourrée fantasque*. The central waltz section belongs, however, to the world of fashionable French ballet music.

1889 also saw the composition of the *Fantaisie* for piano and orchestra, discussion of which more properly belongs to a book on

[1] *Claude Debussy: his life and works* (London, 1933).

16

Debussy's orchestral music. The dissatisfied composer withheld it during his lifetime. Then follows a group of six separate pieces (excluding the *Suite bergamasque* for the moment) attributable, though not always with certainty, to the years 1890 and 1891. They are of variable quality, seeming on the whole less assured than the *Arabesques* and *Petite Suite,* interesting less for themselves, perhaps, than for the light they throw on the sources of Debussy's early piano style.

Rêverie was published in 1890, but is certainly a good deal earlier, for at the time of its publication Debussy wrote to Fromont the publisher:

I regret very much your decision to publish *Rêverie* . . . I wrote it in a hurry years ago, purely for material considerations. It is a work of no consequence and I frankly consider it absolutely no good.

But it has its champions and it has its points of interest. Tonality is ambiguous at the outset, a melody in F being floated over a subdominant pedal and broken-chord accompaniment with a strong gravitation towards supertonic harmony. The feeling of tonal suspense (the tonic chord is reached unambiguously only in the ninth bar) is well fitted to the conception of a reverie, and the result is faintly modal in a way that recalls Fauré. But the style is not consistent, and soon it is Borodin of whom one is reminded:

Ex. 6

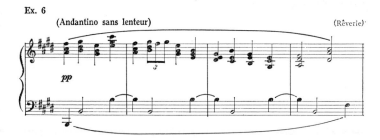

The *Ballade* was originally published as *Ballade slave* in 1890 and the qualifying adjective was dropped only when the piece was re-issued in 1903. That adjective, however, gives a clue to the character of the piece and the kind of influences that went to its making. It is almost entirely monothematic, based on a melody with much monotonous repetition of figures (a feature of Russian folk-music)

mainly concerned with the smaller intervals. Unusually for Debussy, the piece is constructed on the variation principle. Despite
the Russian flavour of the theme, the pianistic lay-out more often
recalls the early style of Fauré, though there is a slight hint of
Debussy's great sea music in the *animez peu à peu* section with its
wide-flung left-hand arpeggios.

Danse is another piece published in 1890 that took on a new,
more uncommittal title when reissued in 1903. (It had originally
been known as *Tarantelle styrienne*.) This is quite the most completely satisfactory piece of this group of six. Cortot suggests that
it creates sensations rather than sentiments, thus looking forward
to the impressionist pieces of 1903 onwards. After a joyous opening, suggestive of Chabrier in its hedonistic abandonment to
pleasure and in which there is a constant tug-of-war between
3/4 and 6/8 rhythm, the piece settles finally for a regular 6/8 and
the modest prototype of the Debussyan toccata is born. Out of
a groundwork of rapid, pattering repeated notes, tiny scintil-
lating chords are thrown up, often in a fragmentary sort of way.
Intersecting hands produce thrumming effects rather like those
used later to simulate the guitar. Melodies have still a slightly
Russian cast, and there is a brief moment when Debussy surely had a
dim vision of the restlessly rolling waves of *La Mer,* born perhaps
out of Rimsky-Korsakov's recently composed *Sheherazade*:

Ex. 7

The *Valse romantique* was also published in 1890, though the complete absence of anything remotely Debussyan in its manner suggests an earlier date of composition. It is a remote descendant of Chopin, and a certain general graciousness and a few nice touches of scoring are its only virtues. There is no feeling here that Debussy is even peering forward into the twentieth century. *Nocturne*, yet another piece published in 1890, is again entirely in the style of the romantics. The plural is used advisedly, for this odd piece begins with Lisztian flourishes for five bars, Debussy's most distinctive contribution being the pianissimo indication at the outset, followed by a languorous melody *à* la Massenet, which gives place in turn to a few bars of mechanical rising sequences that could easily pass for Grieg. And a passage of quasi-recitative later, which is marked *dans le caractère d'une chanson populaire,* has a flavour of the folk-based style of Borodin or Rimsky-Korsakov even to its modal triadic harmony at the cadence. A little further on there is a touch of Wagnerian chromaticism for virtually the only time in these early piano works:

Ex. 8

(Allegretto)   (Nocturne)

Altogether a mixed bag, but the ending has a shimmering delicacy not unworthy of the composer.

Mazurka, the last piece of this group, was published in 1891. Like the *Valse romantique*, it is distantly related to Chopin, especially in its rhythmic details, in accompanimental patterns, and in the use of an inflected scale. Again, soon after the *risoluto* indication, there are some rather laboured Griegian sequences. There is no adventurousness in the keyboard writing and altogether little of real interest.

Marche écossaise sur un thème populaire for piano duet was the result of an odd commission. Lockspeiser gives an amusing account of the circumstances leading to its composition:

At his humble lodgings, about 1891, Debussy received a call, unannounced, from a distinguished Scottish officer, General Meredith Reid. Speaking not a word of French, he thrust before the bewildered composer his elegant visiting card. Composer and general thereupon faced each other in a dumb-show of perplexity, until an interpreter was discovered in a nearby tavern, where the commission was happily received to arrange and orchestrate a march traditionally associated with the general's ancestors, the ancient Earls of Ross, known also as the Lords of the Isles. The original edition ... bore the title, *Marche des anciens comtes de Ross, dédiée à leur descendant le général Meredith Reid, grand'croix de l'ordre royal du Rédempteur*.

Although it was orchestrated in due course, the piece goes well as a piano duet. The melody supplied by the general is a lively, modal bagpipe tune, and the drone of the pipes is suggested, not by means of the usual open fifth in the bass, but by compound trills on an augmented triad.

With the possible exception of *Danse* and the *Menuet* of the *Petite Suite,* something of the spirit of the Verlaine songs spills over into the piano music for the first time in the *Suite bergamasque.* The connection is explicit in the title. This is the world of Verlaine's *masques et bergamasques,* the world of Harlequin and Columbine, of Pierrot and Punchinello; of the Italian players who played the parts in the *commedia dell'arte,* so popular in Paris in the time of the great French *clavecinistes.* That world was limned by their contemporary Watteau, who, in his greatest paintings, added to its surface gaiety overtones of the melancholy that clouded the latter years of the reign of Louis XIV. Such a painting as the 'Arlequin et Columbine' in the Wallace Collection in London is rich in the ambiguity that lies at the root of so much great art. Harlequin, behind his black mask, woos a not unwilling Columbine. Behind them, dimly perceived in the heavy shadow of a background arbour, is a severe-looking, armless classical statue, to which the actors pay no attention. This is the world of Mellers's 'mask and phantom', the world to which Verlaine looked back with bitter-sweet nostalgia, a nostalgia that was perhaps most perfectly realised in music in Fauré's superb setting of 'Clair de lune', but which was captured memorably enough by Debussy on many occasions. In the piano music one aspect of his preoccupation with the 'mask and phantom' is, of course, his frequent use of dance-forms, toccatas and toccata-type preludes derived from the *clavecinistes.* In the *Suite bergamasque* there are three such things; *Pour le piano* is wholly devoted to such forms, and isolated examples turn up from time to time in the later works.

The *Suite bergamasque* begins in rather unpromising fashion with a *Prélude* that goes back to the style of the *Arabesques* in the main, even to the extent of certain thematic resemblances with the second of them. There are even one or two Grieg-like sequences. But there is, at bar 20, a charming moment of coquetry that is just enough to keep the *Prélude* in touch with the character of Columbine. The *Menuet* conveys, far more clearly than the *Prélude*, the spirit of Verlaine's *masques et bergamasques*. Its atmosphere of dreamlike unreality is helped by textures as delicate as, and more fanciful than, those in the *Menuet* of the *Petite Suite,* and by an A minor tonality kept extremely fluid by means of modal features and the avoidance of the more orthodox chord-progressions. The tonic chord itself is hardly touched until the first clear perfect cadence in bars 17–18. Particularly delightful is the ending, with its touch of breathlessness in the fragmented rhythms and its ghostly *glissando* vanishing into the darkness.

The darkness is softly illumined in the next piece, the silvery *Clair de lune*. The title possibly comes from Verlaine's poem of the same name, in which he has a vision of long-dead dancers in the moonlight dancing forever to a ghostly music, though there is not much dance element in Debussy's piece. The lovely opening has a static quality, hanging in mid-air as it were, achieving the slowest of descents over the first eight bars – a descent symbolical, one feels, of the gentle shedding of light from the moon's rays. *Clair de lune* is another piece with a shadowy and memorable ending in which one of the main themes is reduced to the merest fragments, embodying, too, an unusual and distinctive cadence. There are also some mild pointers to the future. From the section beginning with bar 15 it is a short step to Debussy's typical use of consecutives in his later work. And at the return of the main theme towards the end (*a tempo primo*) there is the merest hint of the composer's later preoccupation with the theories of acoustics. The broken-chord patterns here are orthodox enough, but it is clear that Debussy is concerned to produce something of the shimmering effect of overtones over soft, bell-like fundamentals in the middle register.

In the final *Passepied* Debussy comes nearer to the style of the *clavecinistes* than hitherto. It is a pastiche which may derive from such a work as Delibes' *Le roi s'amuse* as much as from original sources. Whatever the case, the result is a charming piece in which wistfulness and gaiety mix in about equal measure. Debussy cannot quite bring himself to omit the minor third in the final chord, but there are enough open fifths in the last ten bars to give the short coda a decidedly prophetic air.

The four pieces of the *Suite bergamasque* were composed in 1890, though publication was held up until 1905. After their composition Debussy brought no more piano works to completion until April 1901, when two works each added a facet or two to his existing piano style, one extending the geographical boundaries of his world, the other bringing for the first time into his piano music the harmonic concepts that were to be part of his stock-in-trade for the remainder of his career. *Lindaraja,* for two pianos, is notable as the first Debussy piece to incorporate Spanish rhythms and idioms. There are interesting harmonic features too: chains of consecutive triads, the free use of the major second as a harmonic unit, and melodies, some based on arbitrary scales, showing a firm grasp of Andalusian forms of musical speech:

Ex. 9

The title-page of *Pour le piano* carries the date January–April 1901. Evidence that new ideas were penetrating Debussy's piano style some years before this exists, however, in the shape of early versions of the *Sarabande* from this suite, and of *Jardins sous la pluie* from *Estampes,* which formed part of four *Images* composed (though never published) in 1894. *Pour le piano* has rightly been considered a key work in the composer's development. It has much of the spirit of the Watteau–Verlaine *fêtes galantes* world and goes back to the *clavecinistes* for its forms, which are handled with a regard for classical ideas of proportion not so plainly in evidence in Debussy's impressionist pieces. It is at the same time the first keyboard work to exhibit to any degree elements of the essentially Debussyan harmonic language: discords not resolving but moving in chains, their intervals unaltered; whole-tone scales, pentatonic and arbitrary scales, and touches of tonal ambiguity. The magnificent opening theme of the *Prélude* has its clear A minor clouded as early as the second bar, where a delightful chromatic upward slither recalls the accompaniment to the song 'Fantoches' in the first set of *Fêtes galantes*:

Ex. 10

Assez animé et très rhythmé   (Pour le Piano : Prélude)

an accompaniment that is as fully in the Debussyan toccata style as this *Prélude*. Surprisingly, the *Prélude* is cast in a form resembling that of the classical sonata, with the wonderful broad melody beginning in bar 6 playing, though in the tonic key, the part of second subject, and the reference back to the opening by means of the big consecutive chords on page 4 constituting a codetta to the exposition. The whole-tone scale at the foot of that page plunges into a thoroughgoing development where ascending sequences show little trace of their possible origin in Grieg. The delicate right-hand triplets of this section bring a note of fantasy, of the masquerade, though they may derive from the sounds of the *gamelan*. Half way down page 7 a beautifully easy return to a modified recapitulation is engineered. The *Prélude* ends with a remarkable harplike cadenza, with modal and whole-tone scales alternating.

The grave *Sarabande* is also highly formal in design and regular in its phraseology. It has been suggested that the chains of consecutive sevenths and ninths have their origin in Satie's *Sarabandes* of 1887. Debussy's more varied piece has certainly a similarly archaic flavour. The brilliant *Toccata* is Debussy's most pianistically virtuosic piece to date. The right-hand arpeggios of the delicately syncopated middle section, though by no means prohibitive, suggest that Debussy will soon be calling for the utmost virtuosity in his pianists. The *Toccata* is, like its companions, clear in form and texture, but it has much harmonic interest. Much of it is diatonic, but modal elements are always elbowing their way in, and one has to look no further than the third bar for a fragment of pentatonic scale:

Ex. 11

(Pour le Piano : Toccata)

Most of the typical elements of Debussy's style had by now reached the piano music, and he was ready to deploy them on a richer, more ambitious scale. The first fruits of his new-found pianistic strength were the *Estampes* of 1903.

III
1903–1913

With the exception of *Clair de lune,* all the pieces discussed in the previous chapter have non-pictorial, more or less non-committal titles – or, if they commit the composer to anything, it is, at most, to a generalised sentiment or notion. Now he was to change course. Not counting *La boîte à joujoux*, a ballet that it was no doubt intended from the first to orchestrate, Debussy composed 45 piano pieces in the decade 1903–13, all but some half-dozen of them with titles evocative of specific scenes, sounds, or even scents. His perfected piano style made possible miracles of subtle suggestion, but even if much was gained, something was lost in the process. One point of view was vigorously put by Wilfrid Mellers:

The so-called impressionistic piano pieces are often too much like the raw material out of which art might be made, so passively sensory as to be hardly worth calling art at all . . . Debussy . . . cares only for the moods and vibrations of sensation which they produce in him . . . These pieces express only a tiny fraction of Debussy's personality: they illustrate his remarkable and delicate nervous sensibility, but they contain almost nothing of his unique vision . . . Of course there are exceptions, . . . notably the magnificent *L'Isle joyeuse* and some of the Spanish pieces.[1]

This may seem an extreme view, but it contains more than a germ of truth. The delicate sentiment of the songs and, to a lesser degree, of the *Suite bergamasque* tends, from 1903, to be diverted away from the piano music and to be replaced by pure sensation. That fact – the general objectivity in the recording of impressions picked up by the acutely sensitive nerves, the sensitised antennae of the composer – is, however, a factor, though in some ways a limiting one, that goes far to explain the unique character of the piano music of 1903–13. Whatever precedent Debussy had leaned on hitherto is almost completely assimilated in a wholly personal style. He is now out on his own.

The great expansion of pianistic resource that is observable in the *Estampes* of 1903 was perhaps a logical enough development for a composer who was himself a good pianist, and who had already shown considerable mastery in the orchestral field. But a fillip may have been given by the publication, twelve or so months before, of Maurice Ravel's *Jeux d'eau*, a work that fuses neo-Lisztian techniques with pictorialism of a sensitive, impressionist kind. Ravel grew a little impatient of the praise lavished on Debussy by the critic Pierre Laloy, and wrote to the latter:

You propound at length on a rather special kind of piano writing, the invention of which you ascribe to Debussy. But *Jeux d'eau* appeared at the beginning of 1902, when the only known works of Debussy were the three pieces forming the suite *Pour le piano* which, I need hardly say, I deeply admire, but which from a purely pianistic viewpoint conveyed nothing really new.

Pagodes, the first of the *Estampes*, illustrates Debussy's new atti-

[1] *Op. cit.* This paragraph and the quotation on pp. 6–7 were omitted from a revised version of the article in the author's *Studies in Contemporary Music* (London, 1947).

tude. It is essentially a still picture. What appears on the page to be an element of rhythmic propulsion only succeeds in turning in on itself in a series of slow rotations. The static feeling is partly due to the free use of long pedal-points, partly to an almost constant preoccupation with a pentatonic melodic organisation precluding any sense of harmonic movement. There is, however, considerable variety in the way Debussy handles pentatonic fragments: to produce delicate arabesques (bar 3 etc.), in two-part counterpoint (bar 11 etc.), in a sort of inward-turning canon (bar 23 etc.), harmonised in fourths and fifths (bar 27 etc.) and as a more richly harmonised undertow to the *gamelan* tinklings quoted in Ex. 4. The 'rather special kind of piano writing' referred to by Ravel is most obviously present in the elaborate filigree decoration of the latter part of the piece. The contrapuntal features of *Pagodes* recall Debussy's remark that 'even Palestrina's counterpoint is child's play when compared with that found in Javanese music'. This, his first dream of the orient, was plainly given its impetus by that music.

Sentiment does not entirely disappear from the piano music of the impressionist years. Where it is still to be found is usually in pieces associated with the Watteau–Verlaine dream, or in pieces inspired by the composer's new enthusiasm for the music of Spain. The Spanish pieces are mostly nocturnal, dark and sorrowing, even verging on the tragic in their restrained intensity of feeling. *Lindaraja* was a worthy forerunner to the first of the Spanish solo pieces, *La soirée dans Grenade*. Falla's enthusiasm has already been mentioned, and there is no doubt about the absolute authenticity of Debussy's use of Spanish idioms. Basic to the piece is an *ostinato* based on the rhythm of the *habanera,* but despite the almost constant presence of this feature there is no feeling of the static quality of *Pagodes*. Beginning and ending in almost complete silence, the body of the piece is beautifully shaped to its climaxes. Thematic material encompasses a wide variety of mood and style, ranging from a morose Moorish chant, in which much play is made with an 'oriental' augmented second, to the extrovert, foot-stamping dance-song (a distinctly popular element) at *très rhythmé*. Debussy's theory that major and minor modes were not really separable but should coexist in a flexible way, is well illustrated at several points: very simply at bar 52 and in a more complex way just before the indication *très rhythmé*:

Ex. 12

(Mouvement de Habanera)   (La soirée dans Grenade)

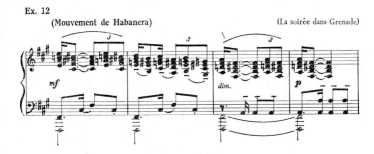

Such a passage as this raises acute problems of pedalling. If the sustaining pedal is used entirely in accord with the bass minims some degree of confusion results. Yet the presence of those minims suggests that Debussy wanted a hazy blurring. Some astute half-pedalling may be the answer in this and many similar cases in his music. *La soirée dans Grenade* is a good example of what I have earlier described as 'a counterpoint of subject matter'. Apart from the extremely contrasted themes mentioned above, all sorts of sounds flit in and out of the texture as they are picked up by the composer's imaginative inner ear: thrumming guitars very briefly at *tempo giusto* near the beginning and, even more fleeting, what must surely be the sounds of far-off castanets at *léger et lointain* near the end. The piece fades out with a superbly evocative coda distilling all the sadness inherent in the Moorish theme and picking up, as if from afar, the last few twangs of a guitar.

Jardins sous la pluie, the third of the *Estampes,* is another Debussy-an toccata, having something in common with the *Prélude* of *Pour le piano* which, in its original form, it may have antedated. The picture is obviously that of a child looking out from a nursery window at the rain drenching the garden, for two well-known French nursery songs are woven into the music's texture: 'Do, do, l'enfant do' and 'Nous n'irons plus au bois'. These tunes to some extent determine the piece's main melodic outlines as they are pressed into modal and chromatic harmonic contexts. For the rest, the rain splashes about with varying intensity, sometimes falling lightly, sometimes dashed in furious gusts against the window pane.

Another short piece belongs to 1903. *D'un cahier d'esquisses* is, as its title implies, a sketch, though by no means an insubstantial or unimportant one. It seems to have more connection with the orchestral music than with the impressionistic piano pieces contemporary with it. As E. Robert Schmitz points out,[1] *La Mer* was in process of gestation at the time, and *D'un cahier d'esquisses* may well be a preliminary sketch trying out some of the features of the great orchestral work, especially of its first movement. Here, at the beginning, is that same wavelike, rocking figure that dominates that part of *De l'aube à midi sur la mer* between figs. 11 and 13. Here, too, are characteristic harp splashes and melodies one can more readily associate with orchestral instruments than with Debussy's piano.

Two fine pieces belong to 1904. Debussy toyed with the idea of including both of them in his not yet published *Suite bergamasque*. That would make plain their connection with the world of Pierrot, even if their titles, *Masques* and *L'Isle joyeuse,* were not so explicit. *Masques,* the simpler of the two, reads like a portrait of the vivacious Scaramouche and is an obvious successor to 'Fantoches' and 'Mandoline' and to the piano *Danse*. Schmitz suggests 1890 as a possible date of composition, but that seems extremely unlikely when one considers the middle section with its pentatonic counterpoint (very like that in *Pagodes*, although going at a much more rapid tempo) and thoroughgoing whole-tone harmony.

If *D'un cahier d'esquisses* has affinity with *La Mer, L'Isle joyeuse* has spiritual kinship, not only with the orchestral style of Debussy in general, but with the earlier *Fêtes* in particular. The piece was probably inspired by Watteau's painting, *L'embarquement pour Cythère,* and is imbued with a truly Mediterranean spirit of carnival gaiety. In its musical ingredients it is almost an epitome of Debussy's style at the time of its composition. It begins with a cadenza judiciously mixing chromatic and whole-tone elements, and recalling the flute of the faun in a more wide-awake way. The dance section which follows has its counterpart in many Debussy compositions and perhaps derives ultimately from *Sheherazade*. Whatever its source, it brings an exciting exoticism with it. Later there are traces of Debussy's toccata style, even some impressionist splashes of water, before a great surging melody, that would not be out of place in *La Mer,* sweeps all before it. That it was associated with the sea in the composer's mind is clear from his direction at its

[1] *The piano works of Claude Debussy* (New York, 1950).

28

outset: *ondoyant et expressif*. These elements and another fragment
of melody centring on the interval of a third are combined in
various ways (at one point with an elaborate right-hand decoration
as in the later stages of *Pagodes*) until even the 'flute' cadenza gets
back into the riotous gaiety of the ending. Towards the end is a
purely orchestral feature in the shape of ringing fanfares reminiscent of the brilliant brass writing in *Fêtes*. Almost the whole of
Debussy is represented in *L'Isle joyeuse*. Certainly it is the least
inhibited of all his works for the piano, 'the most wonderful piece',
thinks Mellers, 'that Debussy ever wrote'.

The first book of *Images* appeared in 1905 and the first piece of the
set, *Reflets dans l'eau*, is far removed from the comparatively
extrovert character of *L'Isle joyeuse*. If one gazes fixedly at an object
for long enough, the pupils of one's eyes dilate, the picture loses
its sharpness of focus, and a feeling of pleasant drowsiness over-
comes one. So it is here. One feels that the composer gazed long
enough into his pool of water to become bemused by the spectacle
of endlessly shifting reflections. They shimmer, dissolve and
reform as he drops his three notes into them with a quiet plop at
the beginning of the piece. A little later, reflections are seen in
conjunction with the solid objects they reflect, musically depicted
in a piece of chordal counterpoint in contrary motion. The picture
is shattered when a stick or pebble drops into the water, and the
reflections go into a tiny convulsion before settling again, expressed
in a musical pattern symbolic in Debussy of eddies and whirlpools:

Ex. 13

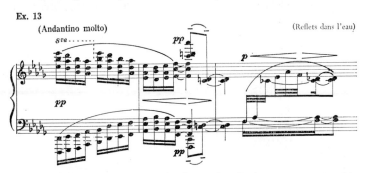

Much of the piece is diatonic, but what Debussy, apropos this
piece, described as 'the most recent discoveries of harmonic chem-

29

istry' finds a place in an admixture of whole-tone progressions (the bass at *en animant,* e.g.), chromaticism and pentatonic fragments. Here, too, is Debussy's new pianistic virtuosity. The glancing lights of sunlit water are pictured in glistening arpeggios and broken-chord patterns. That the Russian influence died hard is attested by a fragment of Rimskyan melody at the indication *mesuré,* sounding Debussyan enough in its context there, but making its Russian point more emphatically later, just before the change to an E flat major key-signature. The last page or so is hauntingly beautiful, and the piece ends in spellbound preoccupation with the three dropping notes of the opening. Of all Debussy's codas this is one of the most dreamlike and hushed.

Hommage à Rameau, the second piece of the set, is a grave sarabande, more rhythmically flexible and expansive than that in *Pour le piano,* but springing from the same impulse to look back to a somewhat idealised eighteenth-century world. Not that the piece is in any sense a pastiche. Rather is it in the tradition of the *tombeau,* a belated funerary offering to one great composer written entirely in the idiom of another. In the main it has an impressive austerity; there are even a few traces of Satie-like plainness in the solemn tread of triadic chords. But, as so often in the pieces that look back to the time of the *clavecinistes,* there is a feeling of emotional commitment expressed through chromatic harmony of considerable warmth. Once or twice a momentary sweetness creeps in rather at odds with the prevailing seriousness of tone. At one point, for instance, Debussy uses major sevenths in a way that became a mannerism in Ravel when he wanted to charm:

Ex. 14 (Hommage à Rameau)

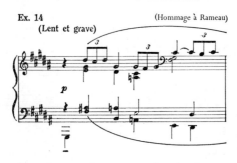

But, as ever, the solemn coda sums up the piece's essential gravity with a slow-stepping downward modal and chordal scale stretching over an octave and a half then coming to rest with absolute finality.

The *Mouvement* of the title of the third piece is largely illusory, or at most on the surface. It is the rapid yet restricted movement of the wasp round the honey-pot, the bird in the cage, of the fluttering wings of the nearly stationary dragonfly. For all its incidental activity, *Mouvement* is locked to immensely long pedal-points that give the harmony an essentially static quality. There is, for instance, a C pedal or inner pedal or inverted pedal present or implied in every one of the first 62 bars, or practically four pages, of the piece. There is a constant shimmer and subtle change of tone-colour over these long fixed points. As Anthony Cross has said:[1] 'With Debussy rhythm is frequently reduced to a continual vibration . . . to permit, as it were, the realisation of timbre effects.' *Mouvement* is a *tour de force* as enigmatic as the finale of Chopin's B flat minor sonata.

The second set of *Images* appeared in 1907. All three pieces are set out on three staves, a great help to the eye in unravelling their complex, elaborate textures. The first piece, *Cloches à travers les feuilles,* is one of the most beautifully fashioned of all Debussy's pieces. Lockspeiser conjectures it to be 'a study in the contrasts of clear and muffled sonorities, designed to convey the slumbrous atmosphere of an autumn landscape with an illusion of distant chimes emerging from beyond the screen of rustling leaves'.[2] The opening furnishes a particularly subtle example of Debussyan counterpoint, fashioned wholly out of the whole-tone scale:

Ex. 15

(Lent)   (Cloches à travers les feuilles)
un peu en dehors

---

[1] 'Debussy and Bartok', *The Musical Times* (London, February 1967).
[2] *Debussy* (London, 1936).

It will be seen that two inner parts form a near-canon by augmentation. Over them floats a fragment of independent melody. Below and among them the quietly tolling A's suggest the sound of distant bells. The rustling pattern persists virtually throughout the piece, sometimes more, sometimes less agitated; and the bell sounds, coming into closer focus at the centre of the piece, are a constant feature too. It becomes impossible to decide how much of the background shimmer is caused by rustling leaves, how much by the overtones set up by the bells. The effect is enchanting, and the enchantment is if anything enhanced by the pensive coda over its descending chromatic bass.

The title of the second piece, *Et le lune descend sur le temple qui fut,* is said to have been suggested by Louis Laloy (the dedicatee) after the piece was composed. That the subject in mind was an oriental one is clear from a delightful *gamelan* effect that occurs in conjunction with a melody curiously reminiscent of English folk song (a melody which is later detached from the *gamelan* feature and given a modal, chordal accompaniment in the manner of Vaughan Williams):

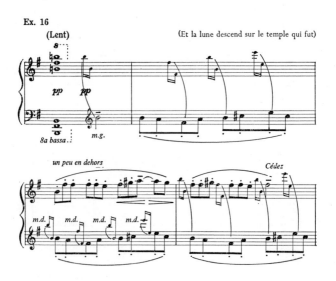

Ex. 16

(Lent)   (Et la lune descend sur le temple qui fut)

For the rest, the piece largely consists of slowly moving parallel chords, sometimes triads, sometimes fifths with an internal fourth replacing the third. They bring a feeling of stillness, of vagueness even.

The *Poissons d'or* of the last piece can be variously translated as goldfish in a bowl, or the golden fish on a piece of Chinese lacquer. Their origin may be in a piece of oriental embroidery or in a Japanese print. At all events, fish they are, of whatever kind, and Debussy brings them to darting, quivering life in one of the most popular of his pieces. Fluttering fins and rippling water are suggested by a wealth of trills and tremolos and by the delicious cadenza at the end. But not all is decorative and peaceful: the bowl (if bowl it is) harbours its tyrant of this fishy world, as the ominous bass octaves beginning in bar 64 seem to suggest. *Poissons d'or* shows yet another facet of Debussy's toccata style and is, apart from its pictorial aspects, a searching technical study. Much of the piece is diatonic or nearly so, and the periodic shifts into more sophisticated harmonic waters suggest the twists and convolutions of the fish in their very restricted sphere of activity.

One of Debussy's *Monsieur Croche* articles consists of a description of Mussorgsky's song-cycle, *The Nursery*. It may have been his admiration for that work that prompted his own *Children's Corner* of 1908, a suite of six piano pieces dedicated to his daughter Chouchou, who was then five, with 'her father's apologies for what follows'. Debussy's little Parisian daughter, already showing signs of coquetry in her make-up, was a far cry from Mussorgsky's children, and there is something more sophisticated, less realistic, about the French composer's approach. The suite contains impressions of the little girl's world and its inhabitants, her toys and dolls. Although Debussy deliberately simplifies his style for *Children's Corner*, this is not really music for children to play in the sense that Schumann's *Album für die Jugend* is. Rather does it align with that composer's *Kinderszenen*: scenes of childhood seen through adult eyes. Neither does Debussy achieve quite the imaginative insight of Schumann, who was able at will to recall in amazing detail the attitudes of children to the world around. Debussy remains the sympathetic onlooker, the indulgent father watching his child at play and joining in her games maybe, but still seeing things from the standpoint of an older generation. The

C

purely musical satire of the first piece, *Doctor Gradus ad Parnassum,* would, for instance, be beyond the comprehension of most young children. *Gradus ad Parnassum* is the title of a great collection of studies by Clementi, many of them – fugues, canons, sonata movements and so on – deeply interesting and rewarding musically, but a number conceived primarily as technical exercises. It is this duller, more purely pedagogic aspect of Clementi that Debussy seizes on to parody, composing 'a sort of hygienic and progressive gymnastics; it should therefore be played every morning, before breakfast, beginning at *modéré,* and winding up to *animé*'. An amusing picture of a child practising is conjured up, beginning with the best of intentions, growing weary and plainly yawning with boredom in the D flat section, but pulling herself together and ending her practice with a great show of *brio.* This, the simplest of Debussy's toccatas, is almost entirely diatonic. There are just a few touches of Debussyan harmony, notably a little sequence of unrelated triads near the end.

Probably in reference to Chouchou's English governess, the titles of *Children's Corner* (and the collective title too) are in Debussy's own rather individual brand of English. He insisted that Chouchou's toy elephant was called Jimbo, not Jumbo, and so we get *Jimbo's Lullaby* next in the series. The elephant is being told a bedtime story, the object of which is made apparent as early as the eleventh bar with a few notes from the nursery lullaby, 'Do, do, l'enfant do'. Later at *un peu plus mouvementé,* the fragment of tune is combined with a few lumbering dance-steps, with which Jimbo goes off into a scrap of whole-tone scale. At last he drops off to sleep, with a couple of notes of 'Do do' still hanging on the air. The interval of a major second is put to much harmonic use in this piece, surely the most light-fingered of all elephantine music.

Serenade of the Doll, which should doubtless be serenade *to* the doll, was published separately two years before the suite, in 1906. The appropriate accompanying instrument, the guitar or mandolin, is suggested, but the prevailingly high pitch of the accompaniment conveys an idea of a miniature or toy instrument. The pentatonic melody of the opening section, with its delicately clipped grace-notes, shows some *gamelan* influence. The more sustained, rather sorrowing melody of the middle section (marked *expressif*) suggests the nostalgia of the adult for childhood.

In *The snow is dancing* Debussy makes fewest concessions to simplicity of style. The free use of whole-tone devices and chromaticism makes for an intricate harmonic texture, and there is much rhythmic subtlety in the middle section. Basically the piece is a kind of delicate chopsticks toccata (i.e. with each hand supplying alternate notes) to which are added fragments of melody from time to time, one of them (at *doux et triste*) either being, or having very strongly the character of, a nursery song. The soundless fall of the snow is suggested in a piece that rarely rises above *piano*, and also something of the fascination and wonder that snow holds for all children.

The Little Shepherd alternates meditative, unaccompanied reed-pipe phrases (a simpler childish parallel to the Faun or to *Syrinx*) with livelier snatches of accompanied dance-tune played on the shepherd's pipe. Although each of the three main sections of the piece ends with a clear perfect cadence, the harmony is progressively complex, a fact epitomised in the treatment of the 'flute' solos. The third of them, with its prominent augmented second, takes on almost an eastern air.

Lastly, *Golliwogg's cake walk* expands Debussy's world to include, for the first time, the music-hall, or at least its open-air equivalent, the seaside beach. Before even that classic, Irving Berlin's 'Alexander's Ragtime Band' (1911), the successors of Christy's Minstrels had made pseudo-Negro American songs (some in the jazzy cake-walk rhythm) popular on English beaches. Confronted with the black face of the golliwog, such a type of music would have seemed apt to Debussy. The result of the suggestion is one of his gayest, least inhibited pieces. There are no subtleties to discuss, but there is one parting musico-satirical shot: a quotation from the opening bars of the *Tristan* prelude with the indication *avec une grande émotion* and a suffix like a chuckle of ribald glee. And so *Children's Corner* ends as it began, with a sly allusion rather above the heads of children.

In 1909 two short occasional pieces appeared. *The Little Nigar* was commissioned for Théodore Lack's *Méthode de piano*, a publication intended to supply the needs of young students. The title was again in Debussy's own quaint English. The publishers have recently changed the title, without, one supposes, making it much more acceptable, to *The Little Negro*. It is another piece in the cake-walk style, much easier to play than *Golliwogg's cake walk,* yet possessing similar features. It is, indeed, one of the very simplest of Debussy's compositions.

Hommage à Haydn was composed for the centenary of Haydn's death, when the Société Internationale de Musique issued a collection of tributes by living composers to the memory of the great Austrian symphonist. Debussy fashioned his thematic material out of the letters of Haydn's name by a somewhat devious process. H is the German name for B natural, and the other two non-musical letters, Y and N, were found by counting alphabetically along the keyboard from A until they were arrived at. The resultant spelling is BADDG, and a theme based on those notes first appears in bar 8. Later it becomes the motivating force at the opening of the *vif* section, the bass of the *doux et soutenu* chords a few bars later, the treble of the right-hand chords a few bars later still, the top line of the crisp chromatic chords marked *animé,* and (in part) the delicate bell-like notes floating above sustained chords on the last page. That catalogue does not exhaust its uses which have, as Schmitz has pointed out, something of the Lisztian principle of thematic metamorphosis in their application. The piece is cast as a slow introduction (*mouvement de valse lente*) and allegro, perhaps an oblique tribute to Haydn's mastery of first-movement symphonic form.

Although it appeared shortly after the first book of *Préludes* in 1910, one more short piece, *La plus que lente,* can conveniently be mentioned here. The *valse lente* was a very popular salon style at the time, and *La plus que lente* is, in Debussy's wryly humorous way, the *valse lente* to outdo all others. Debussy gave the manuscript to Leoni, a gipsy fiddler at the New Carlton Hotel in Paris, where he no doubt picked up the idea for the piece. Schmitz insists that it was meant seriously, that with it Debussy was aiming at a popular audience; to the modern listener it is likely to sound like a particularly biting parody.

The traditional conception of the prelude was of a short piece with no great distracting contrasts, possibly preserving a similar texture throughout, as in many of Chopin's, or even similar figuration, as was often the case with Bach and his contemporaries. Compared with the most ample of his piano compositions, the *Estampes* and the two sets of *Images,* Debussy's *Préludes,* the first book of which appeared in 1910, are for the most part shorter, more concentrated and single-minded. The subjects which engage his eyes and ears are many and varied: Lockspeiser happily likens Debussy's piano to a 'musical telescope' focusing on

continuously changing ... exotic images ... of the Orient, Spain, Italy and (not less exotic for the French) Scotland; as harsh magnified caricatures are presented of the Victorian music hall; as legend, prose and poetry are deli-neated in music; as the mysteries of nature are yet again evoked – the howling hurricane or the swift race of wind over plain; as, finally, the spy-glass having been put away, the artist peers into the primary symbols of notes on paper and keyboard in order to produce abstractions of thirds, whole-tone music and polytonality.[1]

Here, in short, is Debussy's world in little. The first prelude, *Danseuses de Delphes,* returns to the spirit of the sarabandes, though its extraordinarily chaste classicality comes nearer to the vaguely Grecian world of Satie's *Gymnopèdies* and *Gnossiennes.* The grave dance is a religious one, part of the rites of the Temple of Apollo at Delphi. Debussy's direct inspiration may, however, have come from sculpted figures on Greek vases. The prelude is a brief *resumé* of Debussy's harmonic and melodic processes: pentatonic melodies, similar motion chords both consonant and dissonant, exist side by side and often in combination, as at the indication *doux mais en dehors,* where a pentatonic melody goes in counterpoint with a rising scale of major and minor chords:

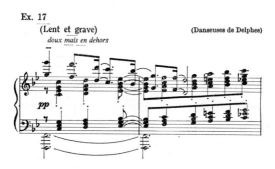

Ex. 17

(Lent et grave) (Danseuses de Delphes)

doux mais en dehors

The Telefunken company have in recent times issued a long-

[1] *Debussy.*

playing record of piano rolls made by famous composers. Three preludes played by Debussy are included, *Danseuses de Delphes* among them. It is a small point of interest that in the extract quoted above he retains the sustaining pedal well into the second bar before allowing of any damping.

The *Voiles* of the second prelude could be veils or sails. The veiled thirds of the opening, faintly suggestive of the Faun's pipe again, could be either; but the rocking ostinato at *très souple* and the hint of flung spray in the grace-notes of the last page suggest a seascape, or at least a harbour-scape. And the one distinguishable melody (beginning in bar 7) is, in its rise and fall, a very distant relative of a much more confident, ringing affair in the finale of *La Mer* (at fig. 44). *Voiles* is almost entirely built out of the whole-tone scale and has the inevitably static feeling of such things, suggestive in this case of anchored boats rocking to and fro on a more or less fixed point. Alfred Cortot rather fancifully sees 'the flight of a white wing over the crooning sea towards the horizon bright with the setting sun'.[1] But many people will surely see these sails as through a mist with no horizon in sight.

Le vent dans la plaine, the third prelude, is almost entirely subdued, yet it is one of the most exhilarating of Debussy's nature pieces. The wind is enough to ruffle the hair, but it never reaches gale force. Only a few sudden squalls in the middle section catch us unawares. For the rest we can watch, without too much discomfort, the grasses and saplings growing on the plain bending a little before the breeze. The wind blows from a pentatonic direction at first, but veers whole-tonewards in the middle part, and drops to nothing more than a breath at the end in a beautifully contrived way. In pianistic terms this is another of Debussy's toccata-style pieces, one of the fleetest and lightest.

'*Les sons et les parfums tournent dans l'air du soir*', the title of the fourth prelude, is a quotation from 'Harmonie du soir', one of the poems in Baudelaire's *Fleurs du Mal*. Much earlier, around 1888, Debussy set the poem (which is quoted complete in Schmitz's book) as a song, and he returns to it again now towards the end of his career as the basis of one of the most entirely characteristic of his preludes. For what could be more characteristic than this picking up by the senses of the sounds and perfumes circulating in the evening

[1] *French Piano Music* (London, 1932).

air? Schmitz translates the poem thus:

The end of the day, but its overtones are carried in the evening air; nostalgic and poignant are the reminiscences of which the senses can still apprehend snatches in the air's caress; melancholy waltz and vertiginous languor enfold the regrets on the threshold of the black void of night, of the despised vacuum which repels the tender heart.

The curving line of Debussy's opening melody is harmonised with unusual richness, a harmony that one can fairly describe as perfume-laden. The effect at the end, where Debussy asks the performer to have in mind the sound of distant horns, is quite magical.

Les collines d'Anacapri are the hills behind Anacapri, one of the two small towns on the island of Capri in the Bay of Naples. This fifth prelude begins with a typical juxtaposition of fragments: first a quietly built up composite chord suggestive of the hum of far-off bells in the air (Lockspeiser suggests cowbells), and then an equally far-off snatch of a lively tarantella. The just audible vibration of the bells is heard again, but soon the tarantella establishes itself and goes rapidly forward over *tremolo* accompaniments. Into the fabric of the tarantella a typically Neapolitan song-melody is soon introduced (in the bass at first, at the indication *avec la liberté d'une chanson populaire*) and another more sentimental and no less Neapolitan melody forms the basis of the slower middle section. The sensuous sway of the rhythm here, produced by following a triplet of quavers with two normal quavers, has its counterpart in Debussy's earliest Mediterranean piece, *Lindaraja*. Soft bells are heard again, the tarantella returns and the toccata-like ending is whipped up to a dazzling brilliance. The piece, beginning almost at the point of silence and ending in a blaze of light, seems to symbolise the breaking of the dawn. Debussy, sitting metaphorically on his hill, had picked up a great variety of sounds as the little town and the countryside around it had come to life. *Les collines d'Anacapri,* with its largely diatonic material, is one of the happiest and most forthright of the preludes.

In the sixth prelude, *Des pas sur la neige,* the almost constant feature of a short appoggiatura in the accompanimental matter imparts a weary drag to the rhythm, as if snow-covered boots are being lifted heavily and progress being made only with great difficulty. 'Those solitary footsteps . . ., where do they lead?' asks Lockspeiser. There is no answer to that rhetorical question. All is desolation in a piece that exists wholly on the borders of silence. Superimposed on the plodding *ostinato* of the footsteps are some scraps of fragmented melody, prophetic of the procedures of a later generation of composers:

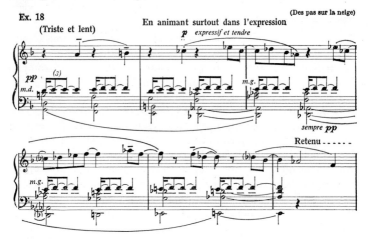

Apart from illustrating the fragmentation of the melodic line, this example emphasises the richly chromatic nature of the harmony as well as providing an example of Debussy's characteristic use of organum-style consecutive perfect fifths. *Des pas sur la neige* is a study in monochrome, the sharpest possible contrast to its predecessor.

In great contrast, too, is the next prelude, *Ce qu'a vu le vent d'ouest,* which demands the greatest virtuosity in the performer. Lisztian features abound: compound trills and tremolos with interlocking hands, far-flung broken-octave inverted pedals, powerful passages in chords and an incisive bass staccato passage (at the direction *serrez et augmentez* near the end) recalling Liszt at his most Mephistophelean. Yet the language is very much Debussy's own, for it makes free use of both pentatonic and wholetone elements. By contrast, too, with the gentler, more amiable breezes of *Le vent dans la plaine,* this is a storm poem, a picture of a dreadful hurricane blown across the Atlantic, wreaking destruction and churning into mountainous waves the waters of that deathtrap for sailors, the Bay of Biscay. There is, in fact, something of a more evil *La Mer* in the restless toss and turmoil of this great prelude. Again it may be noted that melodic elements are extremely fragmentary.

The next prelude brings the sharpest contrast again, for *La fille aux cheveux de lin* is the simplest of all the preludes. The title is that of one of Leconte de Lisle's *Chansons écossaises*, a poem which Debussy set as a song as early as 1880. The young Scots girl sings in the morning sunshine a simple, open-hearted song. Leconte de Lisle's poem (printed in full in Schmitz's book) is formally constructed, with a recurring couplet that gives the essence of the matter:

> *L'amour, au clair soleil d'été*
> *Avec l'alouette a chanté.*

Debussy's piece goes back to the simple lyricism of some of his earliest songs, though the piano piece is quite independent of his own setting of the poem. There are features that belong to his mature style, a modal character in much of the harmony and a free use of consecutives among them. But there is a practically continuous melody along the top of the musical texture, and it is a melody of a singularly unforced, spontaneous kind.

The direction *quasi guitarra* at the outset of the next prelude, *La sérénade interrompue,* tells us immediately that it belongs among the Spanish pieces, a fact that is amply confirmed by the character of the music itself. The dark-toned twanging of the accompaniment deals in typical Spanish guitar patterns:

Ex. 19

Superimposed is a singularly forlorn melody. The lover sounds a poor fish, without much hope or confidence in his powers to charm. Nevertheless, he does just once burst into a vocal arabesque typical of the Andalusian *cante hondo* (at the indication *librement*). The interruptions to his song are treated with sardonic wit. After the first dissonant crash (at *très vif*: a slammed window or even a hurled chamber-pot?) the serenader patiently begins his prelude all over again and carries the song a stage farther. The other interruption is less dramatic – a distant snatch of what might be a popular song (*modéré*) – but whatever its cause, it stings the singer into a violent assault on the strings of his guitar (*rageur*) and for a moment the battle is contested by means of short, incomplete fragments of phrase from either party. At last the singer is left in peace. He finishes his song, but creeps away at the end, seemingly dejected and crestfallen. Once again, in this prelude, Debussy speaks Spanish with the authority of a native.

The next prelude, *La Cathédrale engloutie* – one of the most popular – stands somewhat apart from the rest in that its imagery is made more explicit and it is, unusually for Debussy, a piece of narrative programme music. The very story itself, however, has a mystic, Celtic twilight quality. It concerns the submerged cathedral of Ys, sunk beneath the waves off Brittany some fifteen hundred years before as a punishment for an impious populace. From time to time it is allowed to rise to the surface as a cautionary example to them. Debussy begins his version with a placid seascape with which is mingled the sound of still submerged bells. As the cathedral surfaces the sound of the bells increases in intensity until the whole air hums (at *augmentez progressivement*) with the confused overtones of the belfry. The bell-chime becomes an organ pedal part and a great chant rises over enormously long pedal points. This is at the centre of the design. Another more tenuous melody, based on the earlier bell-music, is heard before everything recedes from view as the chant is heard once again as from a remote distance, with an undulating, wavelike pattern in the bass lapping round it. The piece ends with a version of the placid phrases of the opening. Debussy's materials are varied. His knowledge of the acoustics of overtones is put to good use to create the misty atmosphere of the opening phrases and also for the clangour of bells a little later. There the bell sounds are inextricably mixed with the swaying rhythm of one of Debussy's oft used sea symbols; the swing of the bells and the rocking of the waves are both suggested simultaneously. Medieval organum, as pure as in the eleventh century but for Debussy's added third, is the basis for the great choral chant. His own recorded performance of this piece suggests that he was more interested in preserving the long bass pedal notes there, and at *un peu moins lent* a little later, than in achieving clarity in the upper parts, for he takes the pedal unchecked right through their long durations. Incidentally, he clears up a silly misprint which has persisted for nearly sixty years. There is no trace of a right-hand E in the third bar before *un peu moins lent*.[1]

Following this most solid of the preludes is *La danse de Puck,* one of the most ethereal. This is fairy music of a lightness to vie with Mendelssohn's and a good deal more capricious and informal. A sprightly dotted rhythm set up at the outset is present, at least in the mind, for most of the piece, and forms the springboard for Puck's antics, his sudden leaps, his unexpected vanishings and reappearances, his mercurial flittings to and fro. Ever and anon he stops for a moment at the sound of an elfin horn:

Ex. 20

This horn-call is in itself evidence of the unpredictable nature of Debussy's harmonic procedures. It occurs in various contexts, twice fully harmonised in the middle section.

The last prelude of the set, *Minstrels,* returns to the world of the music hall and *Golliwogg's cake walk.* The minstrels of the title are of the type with top hats, blackened faces and white tailed coats that were such a common sight fifty and more years ago.

---

[1] Debussy's music is now out of copyright, and some new editions have corrected the misprint.

Born around 1828 in the plantations, where household servants put on minstrel shows with Bones, Sambo, and Rastus; cake-walks, cornet solos, scratchy banjos and drums, a sentimental song, a few corny jokes, and feline dances were the main features of minstrel groups which started appearing in Europe around 1900 in fairs, or on the boardwalks of the seaside resort at Deauville.[1]

Debussy's methods here are a good deal more impressionistic than in the earlier piece. *Golliwogg's cake walk* was, but for the *Tristan* allusion, a straightforward dance. In *Minstrels* the whole of the stage act is hinted at in the compressed space of a short piano piece, with fragments of this, that and the other flitting in and out of the musical texture in no seemingly prearranged order. Debussy begins with an imitation of the banjo as effective in its way as any of his darker-toned simulations of the guitar. Soon (at *un peu plus allant*) a plantation dance gets under way, interrupted twice (the first time eight bars later) by the strident notes of a cornet (horribly out of tune the second time). At *moquer* it seems that some mock-grisly tale of ghosts and hobgoblins is being told, but the dance strikes up again more gaily than ever. Later (*quasi tambouro*) the traditional drum-roll accompanies some acrobatics, immediately giving way (at *expressif*) to a snatch of sentimental song. The first collection of preludes ends on a note of rare hilarity.

The second volume of *Préludes* appeared in 1913. Some commentators have professed to find them a little more mannered, a little more advanced in their musical language, a little more difficult to play than those of the first volume. Near the end of the second volume there is an important new departure, a change of emphasis that will be noticed in due course. But essentially the second volume begins as a continuation of the first. *Brouillards*, the first prelude, inhabits a similarly misty world to that of *Voiles,* though here the fog is denser and becomes, indeed, the very subject of the piece, blotting out all but a few dimly discerned objects. *Brouillards* does, however, embody a new technical device, or puts a device that Debussy had used incidentally before – bitonality – to more extensive use. The piece is so organised that for most of its course the left hand plays simple triads in C major while the right hand plays almost entirely on the black keys and a few white-note sharps and flats:

[1] Schmitz, *op. cit.*

44

Ex. 21

(Modéré)   (Brouillards)

extrememement egal et leger la m.g. un peu en valeur sur la m.d.

A short phrase in octaves suggests a temporary clearing, and the widespread right-hand arpeggios a thinning of the mist, but the piece ends chokingly on a diminished triad on B. Who but Debussy could so depict fog in music?

The *Feuilles mortes* of the second prelude, unlike those in Cécile Chaminade's *Automne,* do not blow about in any scurries of wind. Only once, at the centre of the piece, is there the slightest flurry. Rather is this prelude a lament, a distillation of the sadness of autumn, a contemplation of leaves falling from trees slowly to the ground. The mood is very much that of Debussy's own account (quoted on page 9) of his lingering 'in autumn-filled landscapes, bound by the spell of ancient forests'. The glowing, golden harmony consists largely of parallel chords of varying consistencies (triads, triads with added notes, ninth-chords and seventh-chords) and a few scraps of melody, one of which gives rise to a short *ostinato* at *un peu plus allant.*

La Puerta del Vino, the third prelude, is thought to have been a direct response to a picture-postcard sent by Falla to Debussy. The Puerta del Vino is one of the gateways to the thirteenth-century Alhambra in Granada. The piece is probably meant to take in a wider field – something of the life going on before the gateway – for it pulses with animation to the infectious, swaying rhythm of the *habanera.* That Debussy understood something of the contradictions of the Spanish character is made clear by his superscription to the piece: *avec de brusques oppositions d'extrême violence et de passionnée douceur.* The piece opens with a vicious, biting opposition of tonalities as the left hand's D flat major *ostinato* is contradicted by a right hand concerned with a Moorish scale centred on E, an E that has the feel of the powerful Andalusian dominant, despite the presence of an A flat in the ornamental arabesques. The *cante hondo* or 'deep song' of the south is again powerfully evoked. Savage and sweet elements thereafter alternate. An element of bitonality is usually present, a fact which gives *La Puerta del Vino* a somewhat more recondite flavour than its Spanish companions among Debussy's piano works: *Lindaraja, La soirée dans Grenade* and *La sérénade interrompue*. But there is no doubt about Debussy's complete mastery of Spanish idioms in this prelude as elsewhere.

The fourth prelude, *Les fées sont d'exquises danseuses,* goes back to the fairy world of *La danse de Puck*. The texture is similarly fine-spun and ethereal. The fairies of the title flit with dragonfly lightness to a series of delicate broken-chord patterns, trills and tremolos. Some more sustained melodies appear, one (at the first *rubato*) briefly diatonic amid much that is based on arbitrary scales. Briefly (at *caressant*) the fairies dance to a *valse lente,* and on the following page activity gives place to dreamlike wonder, held in suspense by a long, unbroken trill on A lasting for more than a page. The piece ends with a reference to the opening horn-call of the *Oberon* overture of Weber, a composer for whom Debussy had the greatest admiration.

The heathlands of the title of *Bruyères,* the fifth prelude, present a pleasant aspect, even if they are seen a little nostalgically. The piece begins in very much the same way as *La fille aux cheveux de lin* and continues in a similarly simple vein. Some glistening right-hand arabesques suggest, at least to one listener, the sparkling of dewdrops caught in the early morning sunshine. Despite these and other embellishments that render it a little more sophisticated than *La fille, Bruyères* is basically a songlike piece composed in a simple harmonic idiom that rarely departs from purely diatonic procedures.

Back to the music hall for *General Lavine – eccentric,* the sixth prelude. General Lavine (a sketch of him is reproduced in Schmitz's book) is, according to Cortot,

the same old puppet that one has seen so often at the Folies-Bergère, with his coat several sizes too large and his mouth like a gaping scar, cleft by the set beatific smile. And above all the ungainly skip of his walk, punctuated by all the carefully stage-managed mishaps, and suddenly ended, like a released spring, by an amazing pirouette.

General Lavine made his first appearance at the Marigny Theatre in Paris in 1910 and appeared there again in 1912. Somewhere about this time Debussy was approached by the theatre management to compose music for a revue built round the figure of the comic puppet. Nothing came of that except this piano prelude which, as in *Minstrels,* concentrates the salient features of the act into the bounds of a single piano piece. 'General Ed Lavine, the man who soldiered all his life' hailed from the United States and, at any rate in his later life, was owned by Alfred Frankenstein, who commented on Debussy's piece:

But whether it be an impression pure and simple or an impression concocted from music originally conceived as accompaniment to the General's antics, the prelude certainly does convey an atmosphere of jerky movement and fantastic comedy. The little burlesque trumpet-call of the opening, the preparatory bars *dans le style et le mouvement d'un cake-walk,* and above all the marking *spirituel et discret* at the point where the actual cake-walk begins, are Debussyan humor at its best. I find the 'puppet limp' hard to discover[1] but there are strong suggestions of jugglery all the way through, not the least of them being the abrupt chromatic passage in 16th notes first heard in the 29th and 30th bars.[2]

The seventh prelude, *La terrasse des audiences au clair de lune,* is one of the most sensitive and delicate of those in the second volume. There is some doubt about the title. Debussy may have picked it up from either of two sources. Schmitz marshals the evidence:

It is variously ascribed as originating in Pierre Loti's *L'Inde sous les Anglais,* in which he describes the terraces to hold counsel at moonlight ('terrasses pour tenir conseil au clair de lune'), and to René Puaux, French author, in a letter written to the newspaper, *Le Temps.* In *Le beau voyage,* René Puaux, while describing the Durbar ceremonies for the coronation of King George V, as Emperor of India, speaks of 'the hall of victory, the hall of pleasure, the garden of the sultanesses, the terrace for moonlight audiences'.

The title seems to have opened up several avenues for Debussy's imagination to explore. Its source established an Indian setting and the piece belongs with the composer's other oriental musings. Overt orientalisms are few, however, confined as they are to the sinuous, 'snake-charmer' pipe melody at the outset and the delicate *gamelan* bells of the ending. Elsewhere Debussy is concerned to create a soporific effect with drowsily moving chromatic counterpoint over fixed pedal-points.

[1] Perhaps in the syncopations of bar 11, etc?
[2] Article in *San Francisco Chronicle,* 11 March 1945.

Ex. 22

(La terrasse des audiences au clair de lune)

It is possible that the last three words of the title set Debussy's imagination working in another direction: back to the world of Pierrot. There is a distinct feeling of harlequinade about the three bars at *un peu animé*, and it has been suggested that the first few notes of the piece may constitute a reference to the old French song, 'Au clair de la lune'.

Ondine, the eighth prelude, takes its subject from Nordic folk-lore. Undines were water-nymphs who dwelt in lakes or rivers, whose main pastime seems (at least in the case of the most famous of them, the Lorelei) to have been the luring to destruction of innocent fishermen and others who sailed the waters. Others of their number were perhaps less malevolent, and there is not much trace of evil in Debussy's piece, unless in the augmented fifth pedal-point of the middle section or the ominous rising chromatic bass near the end. For the rest, there is naturally a good deal of water imagery, much of which seems to be connected with *Jeux de vagues,* the second movement of *La Mer.* Thus the harp splashes at the opening of the orchestral piece and at fig. 17 are met with in more elaborate form in the piano prelude; the passage in closely moving semiquavers first met with in bar 16 of *Ondine* is an almost exact inversion of the glockenspiel melody just after fig. 25 in the orchestral score; and in a more generalised way the tendency of melodies to rise and fall in a wavelike motion is common to both compositions.

Cortot says of the ninth prelude, *Hommage à S. Pickwick Esq. PPMPC*:

It is quite impossible to conceive of a wittier musical expression than this, not only of Dickens's hero, but also of Dickens's own style. It is his own ironic good humour, his genial wit; every bar of this piece finds its mark, from the comic use of *God save the King* to the snatches of whistling in the last page, passing through all the variations of absent-minded seriousness, diffidence and complacency, that make up the humorous figure which is Samuel Pickwick, Esq.

English critics have thought otherwise. It is not that we mind having our national anthem pushed about; Beethoven did it before Debussy with musical results that were entirely satisfactory, and the tune itself has remained anything but completely stable over the two hundred and more years of its history. To us, Debussy's piece seems to miss the really vital aspect of Pickwick: his overflowing human kindness. There is just a hint of warmth at the direction *aimable,* but for the most part Debussy's portrait is a mere caricature. It may be objected that Dickens was a caricaturist too. But Dickens tended to magnify the salient qualities of his characters, and this Debussy signally fails to do. There are traces of Pickwick's lively good humour and moments where he asserts his authority with all the dignity of the original, but the portrait is an incomplete one. Does the whistling tune near the end bring Sam Weller momentarily on the scene?

Canope, the tenth prelude, goes back, at least for its opening, to the classical world of Satie's *Gymnopédies* and *Gnossiennes*. Canopus was an ancient Egyptian city on the Nile, and it gave its name to funerary urns in which certain organs of the deceased were buried along with the mummy. As Schmitz points out, they were very simple and entirely unornamented but for a stylised sculpted likeness of the deceased's head forming a lid. Debussy's piece begins with simple chains of root-position triads, but something of his harmonic subtlety can be gleaned by comparing the approach (in bar 4) to the tonic chord of D minor (in bar 5 – the piece is in an inflected Dorian mode) with its extended counterpart towards the end of the piece, arriving on the final C major chord with added major ninth. Over this chord are floated fragments of melody that leave D in the mind as quite clearly the tonic. The central part of the piece is improvisatory in style, mostly consisting of the type of texture met with at the very end, i.e. inflected, oriental melodies over sustained chords.

Les tierces alternées, the eleventh, is unique among the preludes in that it takes its being from no external image. In so far as it originates in the contemplation and exploitation of a purely musical phenomenon, it foreshadows the great set of twelve studies that form the major keyboard work of Debussy's last years. Apart from one or two diminished fourths that look like fourths on the page but fall upon the ear as veritable major thirds, only thirds major and minor are used in this remarkable composition. After the tentative trying out of a few random thirds by way of introduction, the piece is organised in a clear ternary form, and the very short middle section is cast in the rhythm of a gracious dance. First and last parts which, for all their chromaticism, are firmly in C major, constitute another chapter in Debussy's preoccupation with the toccata. This is of the intersecting-hands type, with each hand supplying alternate pairs of notes (his other type is represented by *Doctor Gradus ad Parnassum* among other pieces and is marked by continuous rapid passages in either or both hands). Fragments of melody emerge from the notes marked with dashes but, like so much of Debussy's middle-period piano music, melodies are dictated by the harmony rather than the reverse.

The last of the preludes, *Feux d'artifice*, is of all Debussy's works the one in which his own particular view of Lisztian pyrotechnics is most to the fore. Everything is here: close finger patterns with sudden leaps to remote parts of the keyboard (at the beginning), rapid compound trills with interlocking hands (bar 20 etc.), glittering Lisztian cadenzas (at *quasi cadenza* notably), a snatch of soaring melody over wide-flung arpeggio accompaniment (bar 35 etc.), *bravura* octaves followed by great pounding chords all over the keyboard (just before the change of key-signature near the end), black and white key combined *glissandi* (just after) – all these things can be found in Liszt, though in very different harmonic contexts. The whole box of tricks conjures up a vision of a fantastic firework display in a public park, with an eager crowd looking on and applauding. The public park aspect is heightened by a few notes from the 'Marseillaise' with which the piece fades out, accompanied by a last little sputtering jet of light before darkness envelops all. So Debussy ends the preludes with one of the most vivid and, as it was to prove, the last of the visual impressions in his music for piano solo.

A few words must suffice concerning *La boîte à joujoux* (1913), a children's ballet that was published as a piano solo, but which Debussy intended to orchestrate. He even began work on this, but put it aside on the outbreak of war in 1914. After his death the scoring was completed by André Caplet, and the piece was staged at the Théâtre Lyrique du Vaudeville. The main characters are toy soldiers, dolls and so on, some of them obviously resuscitations of the characters of *Children's Corner*. Debussy uses a leitmotive technique lightly and amusingly, and has a good deal of fun at the expense of *Faust* and *Carmen* and the Grenadier Guards band.

IV
1914–1915

The outbreak of the First World War brought a double tragedy for Debussy. The war itself plunged him into a state of pessimism which led to an almost complete cessation of his activities as a composer for the best part of a year. He was oppressed by his inability to influence events. 'I feel I am nothing but a mere atom crushed to pieces in this terrible cataclysm', he wrote to his publisher Durand on 8 August 1914, and in the same letter he said, 'I've got to the state of envying Satie who, as a corporal, is really going to defend Paris.' On a more personal level, too, 1915 was clouded by the rapid development of cancer to the extent that an operation was performed in December. A few months before this he had begun to compose again, and a number of major works – *En blanc et noir* for two pianos, the *Douze études* for piano, and the three chamber sonatas – were brought to completion by the spring of 1917. These wartime works show some change of direction on Debussy's part. On the whole (though there are exceptional passages) the harmonic texture suggests that Debussy was entering a neo-classical phase in which procedures were less arbitrary than in the middle-period works. None of these later works has an evocative, impressionistic title, if one excepts the poetic mottoes that stand at the heads of the three otherwise untitled pieces of *En blanc et noir*. There is an absence, too, of any particularised pictorialism or symbolism in these works, again if one excepts the war-sounds and the symbolic use of a German chorale in the second *En blanc et noir* piece. The character of the late works, and the absence of features that were, in the immediately preceding years, in danger of becoming mannerisms, can be seen to symbolise the dropping of scales from Debussy's eyes, the end of the dream and a facing up to unpleasant reality. But the mood of the two main piano works is very different one from another. The *Études* are, to quote a phrase used by David Cairns apropos the Schubert Octet, 'a reaffirmation of life in the midst of despair'. There is none of that imperfectly concealed, catch-in-the-voice misery that lies just beneath the skin of the late sonatas. In *En blanc et noir*, 'that mournfully vivacious war music', the despair is more apparent. But before discussing these two works, there is a suite belonging to the pre-war months of 1914, as well as a couple of smaller wartime things.

Had the *Six épigraphes antiques* for piano duet been entirely the work of 1914, one could have been excused for seeing in them the final economy of Debussy's impressionistic style. The title suggests an epigrammatic character, and these short pieces are far removed from the expansive *Estampes, Images* and *L'Isle joyeuse*. Yet they are scarcely as epigrammatic as the tiny pieces which served as sketches for them. These were twelve minute pieces for two harps, two flutes and celesta composed in 1900 to accompany a reading of some of Pierre Louÿs's *Chansons de Bilitis* at the offices of the *Journal* in Paris. These twelve pieces totalled 150 bars of music between them. The *Six épigraphes antiques* average about 45 bars each, so it is clear that they have been to some extent expanded and rewritten. The *Chansons de Bilitis* are prose-poems on antique themes, first published in 1894. They were given out as 'translated from the Greek'. Bilitis was an entirely imaginary poetess, even though Louÿs prefaced his volume with a short biographical introduction. The prose-poem form itself gives the collection a *fin-de-siècle* flavour, an impression that is confirmed by the often highly erotic nature of the content itself. Debussy had set three of the poems as songs in 1897, and six more form the basis of the *Épigraphes*. Collectively they represent Debussy's last dream of the ancient world of *Danseuses de Delphes, Canope* and *Syrinx*. His titles indicate fairly clearly which poems of Louÿs belong to which pieces. The first, *Pour invoquer Pan, dieu de vent d'été*, quotes from Louÿs's second poem:

Let us sing a pastoral song invoking Pan, god of the wind of summer.

The poem goes on to describe two shepherdesses watching their flocks. One runs about, gathering flowers and bathing; the other spins at her distaff. An eagle crosses the sky. The shadow of the olive tree under which they shelter turns with the turning of the earth, and they move their basket of flowers and their jar of milk. Debussy begins the piece with a simple, pentatonic panpipes melody, later harmonised in a strictly modal way. The activities of the shepherdesses are clearly suggested in the later stages of the piece. The whole little composition contains not a single accidental – a far remove from, say, *Les sons et les parfums tournent dans l'air du soir.*

The second piece, *Pour un tombeau sans nom,* relates to Louÿs's 56th poem. In the poem a girl leads the writer to the tomb of her mother's lover, which bears the inscription:

It is not death which has carried me away, but the nymphs of the fountain. I rest here under the light earth with the severed hair of Xantho. Let her alone weep for me. I tell not my name.

They shiver as they read and stand there a long time in contemplation. Debussy's piece has the timeless quality that comes of a free use of whole-tone scale in slow tempo, though there is, too, a lamenting chromatic descent near the end (*comme une plainte lointaine*). Economy is again the watchword. Melodies are often either unaccompanied or supported only by sustained chords.

The third piece, *Pour que la nuit soit propice,* possibly relates to the *Hymn to the Night* that is Louÿs's 93rd poem. It begins with delicate nocturnal sonorities and grows harmonically richer as it progresses, perhaps to match an erotic element in the poem. The fourth piece, *Pour la danseuse aux crotales,* is based on no. 114, one of Louÿs's more voluptuous poems, quoted below in full in M.S. Buck's translation:[1]

Thou attachest to thy light hands the resounding krotales, Myrrhinidion my dear, and stepping naked from thy robe, thou extendest thy nervous limbs. How pretty thou art, thine arms in the air, thy loins arched and thy breasts reddened!

---

[1] *The Songs of Bilitis,* translated by Mitchell S. Buck, in *The Collected Works of Pierre Louÿs* (New York, 1932).

Thou beginnest: thy feet, one before the other, pose, hesitate, and glide softly. Thy body bends like a scarf, thou caressest thy shivering skin and voluptuousness inundates thy long, swooning eyes.

Suddenly thou strikest the krotales! Arch thyself, erect upon thy feet, shake thy loins, throw out thy legs, and let thy clamouring hands call all the desires in a band about thy turning body.

We, we applaud with great cries, whether, smiling over thy shoulder, thou agitatest with a shiver thy convulsed, muscular croup, or whether thou undulatest, almost extended, to the rhythm of thy memories.

Debussy's piece has, unusually, no changes of time-signature. The whole is cast in a triple dance measure, too sinuous and supple to call waltzlike. It has an orchestral quality. One can imagine the woodwind in general and the flutes in particular being, in an orchestral version, much in demand for the arabesques of the primo part. *Crotales* are a type of castanet, and their sounds are suggested in the accented staccato chords of, especially, bars 11–14.

The fifth piece, *Pour l'Égyptienne*, possibly relates to Louÿs's poem 98, *The Egyptian Courtesans*. The first section of Debussy's E flat minor piece is dominated by a slowly pulsing composite pedal-point consisting of the complete tonic triad. Over this float melodic arabesques in the composer's typical oriental manner. A dance-like middle section has a rhythmic bass formed out of consecutive perfect fifths.

The last piece, *Pour remercier la pluie au matin,* originates in Louÿs's 142nd poem, *The Rain of Morning.* Appropriately it reverts to toccata-type figuration reminiscent of *Jardins sous la pluie.* At the very end comes a reference to the opening of the first piece as the last drops of rain die away. It is indicative of the remarkably spare texture of these pieces that Debussy was able to make a perfectly satisfactory arrangement of them for two hands, and that the two hands can, in many passages, cope with all the notes of the original duet version.

In November 1914 a project initiated by the English author Hall Caine and sponsored by the *Daily Telegraph* for a tribute to the King of the Belgians from authors, composers and artists in the allied countries, resulted in the publication of *King Albert's Book* and the appearance therein of Debussy's *Berceuse héroïque.* Debussy found it difficult to produce something appropriate. The Belgian national melody, 'La brabançonne' which is briefly quoted, apparently and understandably aroused in him less intensely patriotic emotions than it would in a Belgian. Out-of-tune, distant bugle-calls create a bitonal element. For the rest, the piece moves with a steady, somewhat reverent tread. Shortly after its composition Debussy scored the *Berceuse héroïque* for orchestra.

Another and even less important occasional piece, a *Page d'album*, remained unpublished until it appeared in the Theodore Presser Company's magazine, *Étude*, in 1933. Maurice Dumesnil, its editor, suggested that it was composed in 1915 to be auctioned for a war benefit of clothing for wounded soldiers. In style a slow waltz, it has something of the character of a shorter and simpler *La plus que lente*, without the overtly popular touches that belong to that piece.

The title of the suite for two pianos, *En blanc et noir* (1915), suggests a preoccupation with the keyboard to the exclusion of all outside considerations. Debussy himself, in a letter to Godet, advised him not to 'rack your brains about *En blanc et noir*. These pieces derive their colour and their feeling merely from the sonority of the piano; if you agree they are like the "greys" of Velazquez.' But even if Debussy was, as so often before, aspiring to the condition of painting in these three pieces, he nevertheless prefixed each one with a quotation from a poem. The first piece is headed by a quatrain from Barbier and Carré's libretto for Gounod's *Roméo et Juliette*:

> Qui reste à sa place
> Et ne danse pas
> De quelque disgrâce
> Fait l'aveu tout bas.

Debussy used it ironically and in self-deprecatory fashion in 'allusion to the men who . . . stood aside from the macabre dance of the battlefields, thus confessing to some physical defect'. Marked *con emportement,* it begins in a strong C major, like a more portentous *Doctor Gradus ad Parnassum*. A *scherzando* theme (at fig. 1) brings an element of the *danse macabre*, and later this theme takes on a harsh stridency, screaming itself into the foreground over a gently undulating second piano part reminiscent of one of the prevailing rhythms of *La Mer*:

Ex. 23

(En blanc et noir, I)

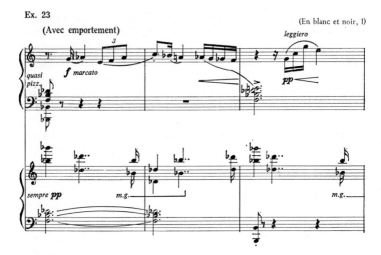

In development this theme is afterwards heard, mixed up with spectral fragments of remote bugle-calls against a gloomy bass *pizzicato* background, before the return of the opening which, after 17 bars, begins to look like a formal sonata-recapitulation, even to the extent of presenting a few bars of second subject a perfect fourth higher. That is one aspect of Debussy's new classicism, and the strongly tonal feeling of the music is another. However, a fierce coda rudely interrupts, and the piece ends on a note of protest.

The first piece was dedicated to Kussevitsky; the third, with some significance, to Stravinsky. The dedication of the second piece to Lieutenant Jacques Charlot is even more significant, for Charlot, who had been connected with the publishing firm of Durand, was killed in the war on 3 March 1915. The second piece is headed by the *envoi* of François Villon's *Ballade contre les ennemis de la France*:

> Prince, porté soit des serfs Eolus
> En la forest où domine Glaucus,
> Ou privé soit de paix et d'esperance
> Car digne n'est de posseder vertus
> Qui mal vouldroit au royaulme de France!

Debussy held this to be the finest of the set. It is the last of his *tombeaux* and the one that comes nearest to tragic grandeur. In effect it is a war scene, though its prevailingly sombre quality suggests a deserted battlefield strewn with corpses and the carnage of war rather than anything more active. Debussy uses, for the most part, diatonic melodies and, for him, plain harmony, though he still makes telling effect with consecutive block chords, notably the six bars of sevenths in the first pianist's right hand at the short-lived *joyeux* section. Bugle-calls float across the air from varying distances. 'Ein' feste Burg' is given a symbolically grim harmonisation dominated by the interval of a second:

Ex. 24

(Sourdement tumultueux) (En blanc et noir, II)

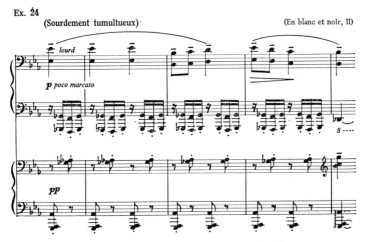

Léon Vallas describes the third piece as 'a simple commentary on a line from Charles d'Orléans: "Yver, vous n'estes qu'un vilain".' It is rather more than that, for the piece does, as if in justification of the dedication, come in places nearer to the neo-classical style of Stravinsky than almost anything else in Debussy excepting *Jeux*. Motor-rhythms abound, in a whole series of accompanimental *ostinati*, and there is something of Stravinsky's sharp edge to many of the melodic patterns. Mellers's phrase 'mournfully vivacious' seems most apt here. There is a springlike activity certainly, with even some typical spring symbols of figuration, but, as Debussy said, it is grey-hued. It seems a spring that, contrary to all the laws of nature, seems destined to recede into winter. Yet there is a hint of consolation in the final *tierce de picardie*, even though the D major chord is overlaid with an ambiguous B flat.

The *Douze études,* also published in 1915, were at first fairly widely regarded as pretty dull fare. Ernest Walker voiced the view of many when he wrote, a trifle cryptically, that 'most [of the *Études*] . . . seem musically overmuch concerned with the narrow matter in hand'.[1] Certainly Debussy based each study on a plain musical fact. But from these elementary premises he launches out into a remarkable series of sound-structures which give, as it were, final meaning to all the harmonic experimentation and all the accumulated pianistic wisdom that had gone before. Debussy's *Études* were dedicated to the memory of Chopin and have at least two things in common with the studies of the earlier composer: profound research into the possibilities of keyboard technique to the limits of their respective composers' knowledge, and the fact that these explorations were carried out in such a way as to produce a highly individual musical poetry. Considered in conjuction with the late sonatas and to some extent with *En blanc et noir,* the *Études* show Debussy to have entered a new phase of his career as a composer. As we have already seen, Debussy claimed that the two-piano work had only to do with 'the sonority of the piano', and, in a letter to Stravinsky dated 24 October 1915, he said 'recently I have written nothing but pure music, twelve piano *études* and two sonatas for different instruments, in our old form which, very graciously, did not impose any tetralogical auditory efforts'. Perhaps Debussy protested too much, for just as it is beyond question that visual and auditory impressions play some part in *En blanc et noir,* bridges are not entirely burnt in the *Études* either. Familiar features of Debussy's musical language are to be found here in plenty, even to *gamelan* effects in *pour les quartes.* Something of the spirit of the harlequinade is present in others, or at least suggested in a fanciful if detached way. Debussy's reference to the form of the sonatas is significant, even in relation to the *Études.* No longer is the composer content purely to crystallise the sensations of his nerve-ends, as he plainly was in such a prelude as *Brouillards.* The *Études*

[1] 'Debussy' in *Grove's Dictionary of Music and Musicians,* 5th ed., edited by Eric Blom (London, 1954).

are, as Roger Smalley has said, 'never a merely arbitrary juxtaposition of unrelated ideas . . . They are poetic music in the strict sense of the word in that they are the product of a continuing thought process which produces a series of images related, not by a background of musical logic which can be precisely demonstrated . . . but simply by the fact that they were generated by that thought process.'[1]

The first *étude, pour les 'cinq doigts' – d'après Monsieur Czerny* is not only a highly sophisticated five-finger exercise, but a parody that has something in common with the *Doctor Gradus ad Parnassum* of *Children's Corner*. Both begin in a firm C major, which is soon challenged in the study by a repeatedly stabbed-in A flat leading to some chromatic caperings and a fresh try in G major that runs into even sharper opposition from a *brusquement* fragment in F sharp minor. Both pieces have C major codas in which left-hand fifths are prominent; both get away into remote flat keys at their centres, the study as far afield as C flat major. At the indication *poco meno mosso* there is a delightful touch of fantasy, a memory of the harlequinade, and the study ends with an amusing variation of the classical pre-cadential Neapolitan sixth in the shape of a D flat major scale of nearly five octaves precipitating itself on to the final abrupt C major chords.

The second *étude, pour les tierces,* also has an earlier counterpart: the prelude *Les Tierces alternées*. As in the prelude, the interval of a third predominates in semiquaver passages, though a greater variety of supporting harmony and more frequent melodic elements are met with in the study. Debussy achieves, in fact, enormous variety within his highly disciplined scheme. With a C major innocence recalling the early *Arabesques* in bars 8–9 replaced immediately by a chromaticism as sultry as anything in Albeniz's *Iberia,* with passages suggesting a more harmonically subtle *Clair de lune* (bars 13–14 e.g.) and, at the indication *leggierissimo,* a piece of the purest Pierrot music with a melodic line as clearly defined as in the early songs, this remarkable study seems to see in retrospect a great many aspects of the composer's career. It is one of the studies that most clearly bears out Mellers's contention that the *Études* make frequent contact with the Pierrot world of the songs, over the heads, as it were, of the vaguer impressionist pieces of Debussy's middle years. *178191*

[1] 'Debussy and Messiaen', *The Musical Times* (London, February 1968).

Fourth-based harmony, allied to a pentatonic melodic line, suggests that the third *étude, pour les quartes,* is going to be another essay in orientalism. But slithering chromatics dispel the notion as early as bar 3, and the study develops as a remarkably free-ranging fantasy confined by no geographical considerations. Even water symbols appear quite early on. A fragment of unharmonised melody (at *l'istesso tempo*), rather Moorish in its cast, is recalled nostalgically and *con tristezza* near the end. In between, a songlike fragment (*sempre animando*) is built up into a strong climax over an *ostinato* based on the all-prevailing interval of a fourth, having here a tonic-dominant flavour in D flat.

The fourth *étude, pour les sixtes,* is a beautiful and reflective piece. For the most part the sixths in both hands tend to move in similar motion at distances other than an octave from each other, thus producing a whole series of compound harmonies. Occasionally, as in bar 7 and elsewhere, the adjective 'reflective' could be used in a more literally musical sense when the hands move in contrary motion, one hand mirroring the other in much the same way as in the passage from *Reflets dans l'eau* already cited in Ex. 13. In a letter to his publisher, Debussy wrote:

For a very long time, the continuous use of sixths reminded me of pretentious misses, sitting in a drawing room, sulking over their embroidery, while envying the scandalous laughter of the mad ninths . . . Yet, here I am writing the *étude,* in which attention to the sixth goes so far as to organise its harmonies solely with the aggregates of this interval, and – it is not ugly! (*Mea culpa* . . .)

The frequent *dolce* and even *dolcissimo* indications are a clue to the quietly nostalgic character of the piece. Something of the spirit of Chopin is here, and the study is in some measure a sublimation of the more tender of the early songs and of such a pre-impressionist piece as the much simpler *Clair de lune.*

By contrast, the fifth *étude, pour les octaves,* is a joyous, uninhibited outburst. Organised in a clear ternary form with a curtailed recapitulation merging into a coda, its E major first section fits Lockspeiser's apt description of the piece as 'a Debussyan vision of the style of the *valse caprice*'. The middle section, though maintaining the triple rhythm of the waltz, has something in common, in its 'chopstick' interlocking of the hands, with such a toccata-style piece as the delicate *The snow is dancing.*

The sixth *étude, pour les huit doigts,* is a remarkable *tour de force* in that it is to be played entirely without thumbs. Debussy points out, in a footnote, that the changing position of the hands makes the use of the thumbs awkward and impracticable. Much of the study, a rapid *moto perpetuo*, is organised in little four-note groups for alternate hands. Tonality shifts often from group to group, resulting in a weakening of any sense of key-centre. In its firefly activity the piece has much in common with *Mouvement*, and it has much the same feeling of fluttering activity within a severely confined space.

The second volume of *Études* opens with the seventh of them, *pour les degrés chromatiques*. With its incessantly whirring demisemiquavers, this study has a more than superficial resemblance to its predecessor at the end of the first volume. But a focal point is provided here by a four-bar diatonic melodic phrase that appears in a variety of harmonic guises and in subtle rhythmic transformations throughout the piece after its first faintly jaunty appearance in bar 11. In its first harmonised version at bar 25 it sounds more portentous, and there is a delightful rhythmic subtlety later when (at *un poco più sonore*) a four-bar version almost exactly presents the original note-values in reverse order. All sorts of derivatives can be found, from the hinted-at diminution in bar 21 to the chain of whole-bar chords beginning in bar 67. The study ends characteristically with the melodic phrase heard dimly through a fading chromatic haze.

The eighth *étude, pour les agréments,* was actually the last to be composed. According to Debussy 'it borrows the form of a barcarolle on a somewhat Italian sea'. Although there is an element of recapitulation, the piece is put together on the patchwork principle of laying short sections alongside each other. The sunny, ingratiating first phrase soon gives place to a short cadenza which is followed by a chordal phrase reminiscent of the *Sarabande* of *Pour le piano*, followed in turn by a delightfully simple C major songlike phrase fresh, it seems, from one of the early songs. And so the process continues. Throughout there is, of course, a high degree of decoration and elaboration. *Gruppetti* are represented by small notes and arpeggiated chords by the usual wavy line sign. Other ornaments are fully notated as, for instance, the left-hand near double trill in bars 11 and 12, and the simultaneous seven-part ornament in bar 38.

The ninth *étude, pour les notes répétées*, shows clearly to what lengths Debussy could bend a purely technical formula to poetic ends, for the piece is at once a searching test in rapid note-repetition, the composer's last piece in the toccata style, and an entirely enchanting fantasy. The stuttering, virtually atonal opening brings thoughts of General Lavine and the music hall as well as a foretaste of Webernian and post-Webernian fragmentation. A hint of the *Minstrels* drumroll and a parody of 'till ready' vamping reinforce the music-hall flavour:

Ex. 25

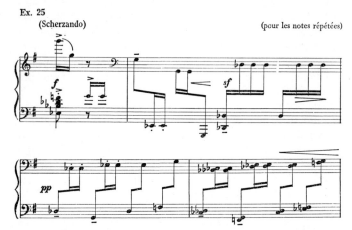

The *moto perpetuo* behaviour of the repeated semiquavers (later even more rapidly organised into triplets) does not preclude the appearance of some lyrical elements, one a long-cast melody, first occurring at bar 28, could well have come from a bitter-sweet song about Punchinello.

A gentle G sharp, which proves to be a pedal-point going through almost the entire piece, with an A natural softly clanging against it, stands as a declaration of intent at the beginning of the tenth *étude, pour les sonorités opposées*. Soon the composer writes *dolente,* and the opening page or so is not so very far removed from the mood and occasional harmonic richness of that most enigmatic of the preludes, *Des pas sur la neige*. Then, over a sustained G sharp in a distant bass register, come sounds of a far-off, unattainable gaiety (*lointain, mais clair et joyeux*), almost like a quotation from *Les collines d'Anacapri* and intensely moving in its context. After a great quasi-orchestral climax, a similar device is resorted to (at *calmato*), with the gaiety even more remote though no less clearly etched, and the single-note pedal-point replaced by a chain of sombre internal chords over a fixed F sharp and its fifth. Apart from the wonderful range of sonorities, this acutely introspective study sounds more like a human, even autobiographical document than almost any other of Debussy's piano music.

The eleventh *étude, pour les arpèges composés*, looks, with its festoons of extended arpeggios expressed as small notes, somewhat Lisztian on the printed page, though its total effect is typically Debussyan. At first slower-moving broken-chords, compounded of never less than five different notes of the diatonic scale, are beautifully liquid in effect. The more rapid arpeggios can be anything from romantically lacy to sharply abrupt and, as so often in the studies, they – the technical *raison d'être* of the piece – prove to be a framework for sustained and shapely melody. Arpeggios exist only as *gruppetti* in the middle section, which has again all the character of a music-hall parody. Rhythmic fragments from this section together with a few wayward arpeggios, scraps of the sustained melody and of the broken-chord from the very opening, are bundled together in a remarkable little coda.

Lockspeiser refers to the 'iron brutality' of the hammered-out chords of the twelfth and last *étude, pour les accords*. The immense, uncompromising power of the first and last sections of this ternary form piece is something quite new in Debussy's music. Though what are academically described as 'unrelated' chords are laid side by side in a characteristically Debussyan way, there is nevertheless an overriding insistence on rhythm, and jagged asymmetrical rhythm at that, which brings us close to Stravinsky:

Ex. 26

Decide, rhythmé, sans lourdeur   (pour les accords)

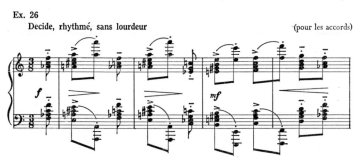

And so Debussy closed his last piano work with a defiant, almost anti-Debussyan gesture suggesting that, but for his premature death, he might have explored entirely new fields in the future. The middle section is less startling with its 'pebble in the water' images and its touches of neo-organum here and there. But the abiding impression left by this study is of an unexpected starkness in which impressionistic illusion has absolutely no place.

WORKS DISCUSSED